Null and Void

How Partisan Politics,
Big Business and Lobbyists
Conspired to Destroy the
American Way of Life

Martin R. Flowers

CONTENTS

INTRODUCTION

On a hot July afternoon in 1776 a group of men stood in a brick building in the city of Philadelphia and took a monumental step forward. Their decision to declare the independence of the American colonies from Britain was not easy in coming. They had attempted to find other solutions, but when the time came where no other solutions were available they knew what had to be done. I doubt any of the signers of the Declaration of Independence knew the importance of the act they undertook that fateful day. They were not concerned with getting rich or becoming famous; they were instead dedicated to standing by their integrity. Our forefathers recognized the problem, understood the risks inherent in solving the problem and in the end realized that solving the problem was worth the risks, even the risk of death, to insure that their own children would not have to face the same tyranny they had until that time. I can't help but wonder what those same men would think if they were alive today and sitting in on a session in the U.S. House or Senate. Our politicians seem to only think of the citizens when they are up for reelection or there is some way that they can get five minutes of time in front of a television camera. What would Thomas Jefferson think of career politicians who do nothing but run political campaigns?

What would John Adams think of professional lobbyists who buy and sell legislation? How did we go from being a nation that elected presidents who were born of meager families living in log cabins to only electing presidents from the "upper crust" of society?

Since 1776 the United States has seen major changes, most of them for the better. We overcame slavery, we extended the right to vote to all citizens, and we expanded a group of thirteen colonies into a nation of 50 states. There have been troubles along the way; we've seen wars, assassinations, political upheaval and the like. But we have never faced a situation quite like the one that we face now. The citizens of the United States are caught between a war on terror overseas and the political hubris that is slowly eroding away this once great nation. The problem currently facing the United States is multi-fold, like most complex problems. And in a larger sense the problems are a sign of how far we have come as a nation. It really presents a quandary, we as a nation judge ourselves based on how far we've come, but it's how far we've come that is the problem. Originally politicians took to political duty out of a sense of obligation. By some accounts George Washington really didn't want to be president. However, he felt that he was the only one that could run the country and bring everyone together long enough to get the nation on its feet. Thomas Jefferson hated politics and was relieved to be leaving the presidency, having run only because the nation was in need of good leadership and sound foreign policy following John Adams presidency.

Now, our politicians are almost always about power. They put up a good front, but the veil which hides their true intentions slowly fads and we begin to see the truth. In truth I think many politicians start out with noble intentions, and then slowly over time the demon that is politics drains all the virtue out of them. They become power hungry, and all they can see is the desires of their political party for more power. The will of the party becomes greater than the will of the individual, they almost stop thinking.

There is a famous quote by the German philosopher Friedrich Nietzsche that says, "He who fights with monsters might take care lest he thereby become a monster. And if you gaze for long into an abyss, the abyss gazes also into you." While I don't agree with much that Nietzsche said, I think that this quote is very descriptive of the current situation in the United States. Since the founding of our nation we have been to some degree obsessed with the idea of preventing tyranny. We spent the better part of the last century fighting Communism. We built weapons capable of destroying the planet many times over and we accused our own citizens of conspiring against the United States. However, in the process of fighting our monster we ended up letting the ideals so fundamental to democracy begin to slip away.

It's not that politicians are bad people, or that they want to destroy the nation. They are simply misguided in that they become so obsessed with power that the needs of the public

4

are no long within their field of view. As stated they are idealistic at the beginning of their political careers, but by the time they go from being a junior congressional delegate to being a major party leader they have undergone a change that seems to be inherited within the hallowed halls of Washington D.C. and most state houses around the county.

The best example of how far we have slipped as a nation can be seen in the preamble to the United States Constitution. The preamble lays out a clear purpose for the system of government that was established by our forefathers. The government is in place to perform five basic functions for the citizens: "...*establish Justice, insure domestic Tranquility, provide for the common Defense, promote the general Welfare and secure the Blessing of Liberty to ourselves and our posterity...*" The problem is our government is not following through on any of these five requirements. The problem is further compounded by the fact that a largely two party system has developed in the United States which allows political squabbles to draw attention away from the real problems at hand. Add to this news media coverage which focuses on reporting the activities of the very vocal extreme fringes of both parties. The result of all of these factors is a nation which is being held hostage by politicians dedicated to keeping the status quo despite the fact that the system has failed. One could easily say that the average United States citizen is suffering from a form of Stockholm syndrome when it comes to politics and public involvement.

We have been told time and again since we were children that the government we have is the best available. It reminds me of Dr. Pangloss from Voltaire's *Candide*, who always says "this is the best of all possible worlds". However, I personally refuse to believe the current state of dysfunctional government

5

which is in place is anything close to the best possible. Maybe it's because of my Christian upbringing that I hold out hope for something better. Maybe it's being descended from ancestors who fought in the revolution which makes be believe in a cause some believe to be dead. What ever the reason, I for one refuse to go on under the false premise that we are living in anything but a plutocracy ruled by the wealthiest members of society. Can we really expect elected officials who live in mansions behind security gates to connect with the people who elect them?

The Constitution is more than just a document that lays out the role of government. In many ways it is the vision our forefathers had for the future of this nation. The document was crafted with clear intent, with compromises, and with an eye for future generations. Unfortunately, our forefathers didn't have crystal balls to see the future. Had they known the consequences of slavery, mistreatment of Native Americans, or other issues I have little doubt they would have made every effort to correct the problems beforehand. Let's face it; it makes little sense to fight a long and bloody war of rebellion only to give birth to a new nation that faces similar problems. If you're going to the trouble to fix something, you might as well fix it right the first time.

With that said, maybe it's time for "We the people" to set about fixing some of these problems.

"...ESTABLISH JUSTICE..."

Let's begin by defining exactly what is meant by "justice". Justice in this context means equality, that everyone has equal opportunities. Now I realize that there are some out there who will argue that James Madison had some other meaning in mind when he wrote of justice in the preamble. Those who believe so are entitled to that opinion as wrong as I believe it to be. To quote Thomas Jefferson, "[t]he true foundation of republican government is the equal right of every citizen; in his person and property, and in their management." The writers of the time make it very clear that justice in their eyes meant a measure of equality. We see this sense of equality in Jefferson's immortal words, "we hold these truths to be self evident, that all men are created equal...". Despite the horrors of slavery and the deplorable treatment of Native Americas, it is clear from the writings of early Americans that they had a sense of hope that the future United States would be one of equality. Early 19ᵗʰ century American writings show people were speaking out against slavery and the ill treatment of Native Americans. They did this understanding the prejudices and social institutions which led to these issues of inequality would not be solved overnight, but would take many generations to drive from our culture. We as a people have made great strides in resolving some of these issues, but there is still much work needing to be done. However, for all the strides we've made, we have managed to fall back in some areas.

We are by definition a representative democracy. We as a nation elect individuals to cast votes on our behalf. The question must be asked then, why are corporations and special interest groups allowed to hire lobbyist to influence our elected officials? The voters elected the representative, not the lobbyist, so why does the lobbyist get more say? Now it's important that we make a distinction here of what is and isn't lobbying. There are some who will argue that the actions of a powerful corporate lobbying firm and a common citizen writing a letter to his or her congressional representative are the same thing. I completely disagree; the only way you can define lobbying in this way is if you're using the definition found in elementary school civics textbooks. A person writing to an elected official or a group like the Veterans of Foreign Wars fighting for veterans' rights is a good thing; it shows citizen involvement in government. However, that is completely different from the banking industry hiring a powerful lobbying firm in an effort to force legislation though so they can make more money at the expense of the U.S. taxpayer. The type of high power corporate lobbying taking place in the corridors of government today is separated from racketeering by the thinnest of lines. In fact, if we are going to hold to the idea of justice and equality being linked together within our society, then how can we not see this form of lobbying as obstruction of justice? It is my opinion that any lobbying activity driven by profit and has no value to society should be illegal. Furthermore, all individuals elected to federal office should be required to relinquish any stocks they hold for publicly traded companies. Allowing elected officials who are making policy decisions to have stock in the companies those decisions affect is nothing more than a conflict of interest. It makes one question who our elected officials are really representing: the people or their pocketbook?

Equality goes further than simply providing for fair representation, but extends to the legal system as well. In addition to hiring powerful lobbyists, corporations hire entire departments of attorneys so they can avoid being held accountable for any negligent action. Corporate America has created a condition wherein they can do as they please with minimal consequences from the government and leave the citizens with next to no recourse. Until such time as Corporate America is willing to regulate itself, we need a government that is willing to go to bat for the U.S. citizen to ensure that our rights are not infringed upon.

I applaud former President Bush for proposing that share holders have a say in the salaries that CEO's make. However, I propose an idea which goes one step further. I propose we make the pay of all elected federal officials equivalent to the average yearly salary of the people they are elected to represent. We also need to stop Congress from voting itself a pay raise. If a member of Congress wants a pay raise then they can earn it by getting the people they represent a pay raise. Now, we would have to give members of Congress an allowance for housing while in Washington D.C.; it's not fair to expect them pay for a house in D.C. and one in their home state. Of course this wouldn't apply to the president and vice president since their housing is paid for by the citizens anyway. Our founding fathers would have been disgusted with the idea of politicians taking office and upon retirement having more money than when they began. To become wealthy while serving the public would have been seen as either selfish, because they're putting their own desires ahead of the public need, or as evidence of corruption.

The concept of equality also extends to having equal opportunities to create a better life. It use to be if you were willing to pull yourself up by your own bootstraps and work hard you could accomplish anything in the United States. However, the idea of the" American Dream" is becoming more of a pipe dream than a reality for many. Equal opportunity means that a person has the ability to work a job paying a living wage, working hours that allows the person to pursue a college degree. We all know at this point the one surefire way to advance your position in life is through education. In a letter to James Madison in 1787 Thomas Jefferson states of the Constitution:

> Above all things I hope the education of the common people will be attended to; convinced that on their good sense we may rely with the most security for the preservation of a due degree of liberty.

Not that a college degree actually allow you to make more money, I made money before I went back to school than I'm making after getting a degree. The importance of education is not making money, it's that an educated society is one that does not fall to the rule of tyrants, be they governmental or corporate in nature. For our nation to have any success in the future we most make educating our citizens a priority.

Equal opportunity also means the credit reporting companies have no say in who gets hired for a job. This issue angers me on so many levels. First, a person's credit score is in no way a refection of their work ethic. I've know some very hard working people who have bad credit scores. Secondly, if a person has fallen on hard times the last thing they need is to be denied employment because their credit score has suffered as a result. Third, and the most disturbing of all, is that using a person's credit report to determine eligibility for employment is nothing more than legalized discrimination. Since women and minorities on average make less money and tend to borrow more, they as a result tend to have lower credit scores. The citizens of the United States deserve to have a credit information protection act exceeding what is already in place and similar in scope to the Health Information Protection and Privacy Act (HIPPA). And the use of credit reports in determining employment should be rendered illegal through legislation immediately.

We also need to hold both the public and private sector accountable in terms of ethics. I will speak more of this later, but this will serve as a short introduction. Earlier I said that we all know the importance of education, however the business community does not seem to share this idea. Anyone who is looking for a job knows that human resources personnel see experience as being more important than education. You can have a college degree but without three to five years of experience in your field you might as well forget about doing the kind of work you trained for. As a field, human resources professionals are unethical and they know it. They use terms like "networking" to disassociate from the clearly unethical practice of nepotism. They engage in free riding activities by expecting others to train and provide experience to potential employees while not providing the same.

How can we expect our nation to grow if the businesses that drive our economy are in reality hurting it? Corporate America is linked to the American citizen. I purposefully use the term "American" because it extends beyond the borders of the United States. Businesses have a responsibility to obey the laws of this nation and any other nation where they conduct business. This means they shouldn't be hiring illegal immigrants, they shouldn't be polluting the environment, and so forth. There are a lot of major businesses right now that are on the verge of failure and it's all because of greed.

While it might seem hard to believe, our nation is in much the same situation today as it was in 1776. The United States has simply traded the tyranny of a royal monarch for the tyranny of many corporate monarchs. The same complaints our forefathers voiced over King George III can be applied to Corporate America. When King George III went to war in Europe it enviably spilled over into the American colonies, prime example being the French and Indian War. We have a similar problem today, where corporations based here in the U.S. go abroad, cause all kinds of trouble and then the citizens inevitably become the targets for what ever terrorist attack some idiot plans as revenge. Of course the CEOs of these corporations aren't the ones who are paying the price. The most that can happen to their company is their profit margin begins to slip; in which case the easy solution is to raise prices on their product thus further injuring the U.S. citizen.

Are we to expect our elected officials to actually do something about this problem? Our government has been in bed with Corporate America for so long there is no way we can trust them to solve the problem. This is part of the reason I support banning elected officials from owning stock in publicly traded companies. It is a clear conflict of interest for the people who are tasked with representing the interests of the citizens to also have an interest in the companies which can potentially harm those same citizens. And no, having members of Congress and the President place their stocks in trust funds is not enough. We need them to completely withdraw their money from the market. If they want to invest somewhere let it be in government bonds.

The interesting thing about justice is that like many things in life it is completely subject to your perspective on what justice is. Congress would argue that they have successfully established justice for those they wish to have it. Unfortunately, that's not what we were promised. No where in the Constitution does it say only certain people will have the right to justice. Quite the opposite is true; we see a document which makes clear the need for justice to be distributed equally among all citizens. For the future security of the United States it is necessary to establish a system of justice that is all inclusive.

"...INSURE DOMESTIC TRANQUILITY..."

There can be little doubt we live in a world today which we perceive to be much more dangerous than we did before September 11th, 2001. The problem is, aside from heightened security measures in some locations and a few thwarted terrorist attacks, I'm not convinced that we are any safer today than we were on September 10th, 2001. A number of years ago over three dozen electronic devices were planted around a Boston and no one noticed. That should greatly trouble all of us. What if those had been explosive devices planted by terrorist, instead of being part of a stupid advertising campaign gone horribly awry? If it had been a terrorist attack the hangers at Logan International would have been used as temporary morgues. The citizens of the United States have the right to live free from the fear of terrorism. We as a nation cannot expect to reach our full potential if we have to continue dealing with people who want to harm us. And I hate to break it to some of you but if this means tightening our nation's borders, than so be it. The U.S. government's first responsibility is to the U.S. citizens, not to foreign nationals. Loosening our nation's immigration requirements and fighting a war against a transnational terror organization are not complementary concepts. You have to choose one or the other; you can't have both and be successful at either. Needless to say we have some hard choices to make. We must provide for the safety of our citizens against threats from abroad and be prepared for acts of terrorism when they do occur. The sad fact is that the death of Osama bin Laden will not end the threat of terrorism.

There are some things regarding national security which need to be understood. First, no matter how hard the United States government tries, if a terrorist wants to kill people, then the terrorist will find a way. Terrorists are just like common criminals in that they look for a point of weakness and take advantage of it. All you need to do to end any doubt about the ingenuity of criminals is look at the various ways inmates have found to kill each other in a controlled environment like a prison. The notion of the stupid criminal is not always accurate to say the least.

There are some "experts" in the field of counter terrorism who claim terrorists are stupid and ill-equipped to actually carry out an attack. The problem is that there are two distinct types of terrorist in the world today. The first type are the ones you hear about on the news after the FBI has arrested them. These terrorists normally have grandiose plans of destroying a building the way bin Laden did on Sept. 11th. However, they have no ability to actually carry out the plan and lack the material support to do any damage other than set off some smoke alarms.

The second type is a very different story. These terrorists are very intelligent, highly trained, and think through the execution of their planned attack in incredible detail. Anyone who has read a detailed account of the events of Sept. 11th knows the extent to which the terrorist planned their attack. The more educated terrorist is less likely to be caught by law enforcement officials. Bin Laden learned our surveillance techniques from the CIA during the war in Afghanistan against the Soviet Union. In addition to being more educated, they are also provided with better financial assets. The Sept. 11th hijackers had money to pay for flight training, apartments and all their other needs for years leading up to the attacks.

Shouldn't the first concept in defeating terrorism be to eliminate the ability to terrorize the public in the first place? How does having a color coded terror alert system help to alleviate the element of terror? Telling the public that you're raising the terror level does nothing but instill fear in the populace. How many of the supposed terrorists have been captured when the nation was on a heightened state of alert? Let's think about this: If we are posting all over the internet and television that the United States is on a heightened state of alert, then won't the terrorist know it also and be extra careful not to get caught? This is just stupidity run amuck. There must be a better way of combating terrorism within the borders of the United States.

One of the problems with fighting terrorism is our law enforcement system is simply not designed to deal with terrorism. Our criminal justice system is designed to only arrest people or search for evidence if there is "probable cause". The law defines probable cause as evidence to a lay person that a crime has been, is being, or is about to be committed. Probable cause presents a problem, since by the time that an act of terror has been or is being committed you have U.S. citizens in body bags. This is the issue that the Bush administration had to come to terms with at Camp X-Ray. We really don't have probable cause upon which to hold these people, but if we don't keep them in custody there is a good possibility they will kill a bunch of our citizens. How does our nation come to terms with an enemy who we can not put on trial, but if we catch them here in the U.S. plotting an attack we can't kill them as enemy combatants? Holding them in a place like Camp X-Ray is probably the best option unfortunately. We can't engage in fire fights with terrorists on Main Street U.S.A. We can't turn them over to some other nation where we have no idea whether or not they will get a fair trial. Our criminal justice system isn't perfect, but at least we can be fairly certain that they will get lawyers and a fair trial.

The Obama Administration's plan to begin treating terrorists as criminals was doomed to fail out of the gates. The first problem we would have to overcome is how does the government put people on trial without disclosing government secrets? Now, I'm not claiming all government secrets are good, or even necessary. However, is it fair to bind the CIA or NSA up in political red tape and other issues when they are only trying to keep us safe? How do we provide the defense counsel with information about the attack which was being planned without exposing the means by which the information was attained? If this is the case, wouldn't it be more beneficial for the government to simply kill the terrorist and never bother with the trial? Our criminal justice system is simply not equipped to handle terrorism, and I really don't want to equip it to do so! In order to equip the criminal justice system to handle terrorism would require the citizens to give up right we shouldn't be relinquishing. Once again, those who hunt monsters...

Even if we manage to put a terrorist on trial and win a conviction, where are we going to put them? President Obama seems content to place terrorists in federal penitentiaries. I must admit the idea of jailing these people in U.S. prisons is scary to say the least. Jailing terrorists in the U.S. will only allow them to further their cause. Look at where imprisoning terrorists has gotten Israel. Hamas, Hezbollah and Islamic Jihad launch suicide attacks against Israeli civilians in the hope of getting their terrorist counterparts freed from prison. Worse yet, we place hardened terrorists in a federal prison with people who are already disenfranchised with our government and can be easily swayed to the terrorist ideology. President Obama's plan will do nothing more than make it easier for the terrorists to recruit from our own citizens. Why bother recruiting and training in the tribal regions of Pakistan when they can do it in Terra Haute, Indiana or Leavenworth, Kansas? The only way I would ever be in favor of housing convicted terrorists in federal prisons is if we reconditioned Alcatraz and sent only convicted terrorists there. The current option seems to be sending them to the federal supermax facility in Colorado, which is extremely expensive for the taxpayers. Once again, there are no good solutions.

I must admit I really don't understand the desire some have with undermining the security of the United States. I will discuss the issues of national security and military involvement in a later chapter, but the issue of domestic tranquility requires a foray into this arena. Since the events of 9/11 there seems to have been a continuous effort by some citizens to defeat every measure attempted to help strengthen the security of our nation. The most popular argument seems to be based on a famous quote from Benjamin Franklin. Franklin said "Those who give up essential liberty to purchase temporary safety deserve neither liberty nor safety." This seems all fine and well until you realize the problem with Franklin's statement. Reading the statement as it is written leaves the reader with the sense that liberty and security are mutually exclusive ideas. Compare Franklin's statement with Thomas Paine's thoughts on the same issue:

> For were the impulses of conscience clear, uniform, and irresistibly obeyed, man would need no other lawgiver; but that not being the case, he finds it necessary to surrender up a part of his property to furnish means for the protection of the rest; and this he is induced to do by the same prudence which in every other case advises him out of two evils to choose the least. Wherefore, security being the true design and end of government, it unanswerably follows that whatever form thereof appears most likely to ensure it to us, with the least expence and greatest benefit, is preferable to all others.

Paine understood that in reality liberty and security are mutually inclusive in almost every situation. If you find yourself lacking in security than you are on some level living in a state of fear, which is hardly conducive to having liberty.

This is the reason that Madison decided to include "domestic tranquility" in the preamble. We as a nation can have all of the rights guaranteed us by the Constitution, but if we are still living in fear what good are those rights to us? We

19

have to learn to walk a thin line here between a security state and a continuous state of fear. One of the best answers to this issue comes from the Bible. In Romans 13 the apostle Paul says "For rulers are not a terror to good works, but to evil. Do you want to be unafraid of the authority? Do what is good, and you will have praise from the same." The lesson here is that if you aren't doing something illegal then what are you worried about if the government is creating laws to prosecute terrorists who are trying to kill you! See, if the government hadn't trashed its own reputation so badly over the last few decades this might not even be an issue. The real issue here is not that any of us as citizens are doing anything that causes us to fear the laws which are designed to protect us. Rather, we have come to lack trust in the government to use those same laws in accordance with the Constitution. We as a nation have to find a way to trust the government we established. Unfortunately this task is much easier said then done.

This brings us to the real heart of the issue of domestic tranquility. Doesn't it seem ironic that the government Abraham Lincoln described as "...of the people, by the people, and for the people..." can't seem to gain the people's trust? If our government officials were really as committed to bettering this nation as they try to make us believe every time elections role around, then wouldn't they be more interested in making sure they do nothing to put the public's trust in jeopardy? This becomes the real issue: how do you "ensure domestic tranquility" when the people don't trust the government to do so? Or is it's even a matter of not trusting the government so much as a matter of us not trusting ourselves?

Once the people lose faith in the government the whole concept of democracy dies. Abraham Lincoln's famous words become of no use because the government really has no interest in the good of the people. Today The United States of America is in fact a democracy in name only. Aside from holding elections every two years that seem to take scripts from side shows and professional wrestling broadcasts, what is there in our society that is democratic? The only remaining remnants of true democratic government exist at the local level where the citizen still has some say in that happens, and even this is being relegated to small town America.

Domestic tranquility must start with the government. If the government is running amuck and not taking care of the people's business properly, then how can the government expect the citizens to have any trust in the government? The only thing that is keeping our government intact and has allowed our nation to avert a civil war so far is the strong economy our nation has enjoyed in the past. As long as the majority of citizens have access to food and shelter and the other basic necessities of life we are willing to tolerate the government we've lost faith in. However, unless the current economic downturn is quickly corrected, I fear for the outcome. Nowhere on the horizon do I see a leader the caliber of Franklin D. Roosevelt who would be able to hold this nation together during such a struggle given the current level of mistrust the government has garnered for itself.

"...PROVIDE FOR THE COMMON DEFENSE..."

At the time the Constitution was written the concept of "common defense" revolved mostly around protecting the nation's borders from the threat of foreign invasion. However, today we realize the concept of defense is much broader and as a result we have taken to using the term national security in an attempt to better define the issues. National security is a very complex topic and impacts virtually every aspect of government policy making. The United States today has without a doubt the best fighting force on the planet in our military. We have shown that much many times before. While Osama bin Laden might have known a thing or two about engineering, he clearly knew nothing of military history. If bin Laden had bothered to study U.S. military history he would have learned two very important facts: 1) attacks against the United States never end well for the attacker, (see Japan and World War 2). 2) When ever the United States gets involved in a war where we were attacked we have a tendency to respond by developing bigger and better weapons to fight the war.

With that said, there is no excuse for our men and women in uniform to lack the very best equipment and training money can buy. We are the most powerful nation in the world, defended by a completely volunteer military. These brave men and women have vowed with their lives to ensure the freedoms we hold so dear. It is completely inexcusable when we fail to provide them with the tools they need to fulfill their missions. In previous wars the United States has been at the forefront in the development of military technology. Like it or not the United States is a nation of war. As many historians have pointed out, as a nation we have spent a large portion of our history either engaged in warfare or building a military to fight a war. This is not to say we as a nation are violent people, quite the contrary. What it does point out is the causal relationship between democracy and warfare. Some individuals have pointed to the 20th century as the most violent century in recent history. It's also interesting to note that as more democracies develop in the world the number of armed conflicts has increased. The more democracies there are in the world the fewer tyrannical governments there are, and as a result those who oppose democratic government will begin to feel they must take action to stop the spread of democracy. This desire to stop the spread of democracy is part of what drives terrorists like bin Laden.

The tools for defense must also include the most accurate intelligence that is available. How can our military be expected to defend the United States if they do not have accurate intelligence on the threats we face? In what was one of the worst budgeting decisions to affect the nation's intelligence apparatus, the Clinton administration slashed the budget of both the CIA and the NSA in order to create a budget surplus. The results of this budgeting decision are evident in that we had no warning of the 9/11 attacks and the fact the intelligence leading up to the invasion of Iraq was so flawed. It is imperative for the safety of our citizens that we make the gathering of intelligence on our enemies a top priority.

We cannot expect to establish a strong sense of national security if we are largely dependant on foreign resources. In the late 1970's we saw first hand how dependant we as a nation had become on foreign oil. Yet, it's over 30 years later and we have done little to develop any alternatives. In fact, instead of seeking energy alternatives, the oil crisis of the 1970's led to the establishment of the Carter Doctrine as the standard for U.S. foreign policy in the Middle East, a standard we are still in part using today. The future of U.S. foreign policy is linked to our use of energy. If we are able to develop renewable, domestic sources of energy it changes not only the way we look at the world outside our borders, but it drastically alters the way the rest of the world views the United States.

The cold hard truth is this, one of the major problems the rest of the world has with our nation is the fact that corporations based here in the U.S. have a tendency to go abroad in search of resources and cheap labor. Unfortunately, in the process they destroy the environment, destroy people's lives, and pay employees next to nothing. Then to make matters worse, when they get caught red handed they run back here to the United States and hide behind our Constitution and government. I have to admit if I were a citizen of another country where U.S. based corporations where doing this kind of stuff, I'd be pretty mad too. As a U.S. citizen I am

24

astonished there are CEOs who believe they have the right to go abroad and make the citizens of this great nation look bad. One has to wonder how many times these corporations have hurt a foreign national and in the process created another Osama bin Laden we don't know about yet, who is just waiting to attack?

I fully realize there are a lot of people out there, both in the United States and abroad, who hate war. To be perfectly honest I hate warfare myself and wish we could all live in a peaceful world. However, the reality is that war is inevitable. There are people and governments who want to cause harm to other human beings for various reasons and we as a nation must be ready to deal with that eventuality. We can deal with these kinds of threats in many different ways. Obviously the best solution is always a diplomatic one. Unfortunately we have to understand there are some people who are so out of touch with reality, and no matter the level of diplomacy, they will try to attack us. An example of this would be Adolph Hitler. Stalin thought he had a non-aggression pact signed with Hitler, but in reality Hitler was simply buying himself time before attacking the Soviet Union.

International affairs are a risk at best and a disaster at worst. The only thing we as a nation can do is conduct ourselves in such a way as to afford us a prime bargaining position at the table. However, our position at the table is based on a number of different aspects. Two of the most important are the ability to project military power and the ability to stand behind our word. We now are left with a new series of problems created by our political "leaders" where the rest of the world doesn't trust our judgment in matters of foreign policy. If other leaders around the world don't believe we have the ability to project military power, then what is to stop some greedy nation from attacking it's neighbors to acquire more territory and resources? We enter into international treaties we are expected to stand behind. How do we stand behind those treaties if there are nations in the world who don't respect the United States? These are the issues which make diplomacy and warfare so complicated. We have to be respected for our military power while at the same time being seen as a trustworthy nation and a good global partner.

There will inevitably be situations where we will have to fight wars. War is a nasty business and not something any nation looks forwards to. If you seriously think a democratic government wants to go to war then I suggest you go see a mental health professional. Warfare is never in the best interest of any nation. In the modern world warfare is generally used as a means of self-defense or in the defense of others and nothing more. Launching an attack on another nation is simply too costly, both in terms of human life and money. In a democracy in particular, to wage war for personal gain amounts to political suicide. The situation the U.S. got into in Iraq was a quagmire to say the least. However, we had few options when we went in and were left with fewer options regarding an exit strategy. Simply packing up and leaving was not a viable option. It leaves the United States in a precariously vulnerable position in the future, both in terms of diplomacy and national security. After taking office President Obama began being much more cautious about guarantees involving troop withdrawals.

While warfare is horrible, the horrors of the current conflict have been somewhat overstated. Let's take a quick over view of the history of major U.S. military conflicts and the casualties involved.

War	Casualties
Civil War	623,062
World War I	116,708
World War II	407,316
Korean War	36,914
Vietnam War	58,169

Compare these figures with the combined totals for Grenada, Desert Storm and Panama where the combined losses were less than 400 troops. Study the above numbers for a moment. Realize that there are some historians who place the figure for the Civil War much high, in some cases close to 1 million troops. At the time of the Civil War we were a nation of 30 million people. In comparison to other wars, the current war against terrorism (if you can call it a war) has not been all that costly. Have we lost some citizens in the current conflict? Yes. However, that is to be expected of a military conflict. The only reason these deaths seem harder to bare is because the nightly news continuously inundates us with the death totals prior to elections.

We saw a similar phenomenon with the conflict in Vietnam, where for the first time footage of actual battles was shown on the nightly news. There's nothing like seeing the Saigon police chief executing a teenager during the Tet Offensive to turn a nation's stomach. So it is understandable when U.S. citizens were outraged over the images of atrocities some of our troops were carrying out at Abu Graib. For many their thoughts went back to those images from Vietnam. In many ways we forced ourselves into the same position we were in during the Vietnam War.

Have we stretched our military to the breaking point? We absolutely have, of this there can be little doubt. However, this is the natural consequence of having an all volunteer military. Having a volunteer military is much better than one which originates as a result of forced conscription as seen in a national draft. With a volunteer force you get a military made up of citizens who wish to fight for their country. With a draft you get some good soldiers but you also get the dregs of society who do nothing more than cause problems. Furthermore, the history of the United States military bares witness that popular dissent is more common when a draft is imposed. Evidence of this can be seen in the draft riots that occurred during both the Civil War and the Vietnam War.

As a student of history, one of the most striking issues to me is the vastly different approach that we as a nation have taken to this conflict. Let's compare for a moment the public response to World War II and the War on Terror. Following the surprise attack on Pearl Harbor, the nation went into a different mindset. During World War II we began rationing everything from food to gasoline. Children were going around collecting tin and other metals for the war effort. Women took on jobs that had normally been held by men. People planted "victory gardens" to help reduce the strain on the nation's food supplies. When we look at the events which transpired after Sept. 11th, something different has occurred. For a short time military enlistment was up, but life eventually went back to normal for most citizens. This difference is not the fault of the U.S. citizens. In fact, we're only doing exactly what our government told us to do in the wake of the attacks. In his speech to a joint session of Congress on September 20th, 2001 former President Bush said, "It is my hope that in the months and years ahead, life will return almost to normal. We'll go back to our lives and routines, and that is good." I wonder what the reaction would have been if Franklin Roosevelt had made that comment instead of say "Yesterday, December 7, 1941 - a date which will live on in infamy..."

The very language of these two monumental speeches is drastically different. Roosevelt is speaking as the leader of a nation which will stand defiant in the face of cowardly violence. The language Roosevelt used was anything but pretentious, the speech was short, but the message it sent was loud and clear: if you attack the United States of America you will face the full force of our military in retaliation and we will not stop until we have complete victory and are assured you will not harm our nation again. Bush's speech was anything but clear, and was ambiguous about how we will proceed after the attacks. We're going to fight the war, but life for our citizens will be as normal. If that isn't sending a mixed message, then what is? Quite frankly, I didn't want to hear about life being back to normal until I saw Osama bin Laden's bullet riddled corpse hanging from Lady Liberty's torch!

I guess the question becomes, how can we expect to win a war if in comparison to wars of the past we're not even taking this one seriously? This highlights the problem; we as a nation have become complacent in the protection of liberty. There are many reasons for this complacency. One of the big reasons is the way war is treated in the media. We see video footage of bombs being dropped on a target and are left with the sense there was never any danger to our soldiers. Prior to the "war on terror" we had been conditioned to see wars as being fought at a distance, from behind computer screens, from massive control rooms in underground bunkers, from the cockpit of an airplane at 50,000 feet.

But once we started seeing the casualty numbers on the raise, the first images within our collective memory to draw on were the images from Vietnam. As a result of those collective images, we began to change the way we reacted to the war, so the reaction was similar to the reaction we as a nation had to the Vietnam War. As the public's reaction began to change, the news media's reaction followed. And finally, as the public and the media both took on the same reaction, the government's reaction took the same course as in the Vietnam War, even to the point of referring to "winning the hearts and minds of the Iraqi people". We saw the images of dead soldiers returning home and a collective reaction on the part of the entire nation followed. We must learn to resist these kinds of reactions. These two conflicts are very different and if we wish to win the current conflict and secure for ourselves and future generations any sense of peace we must recognize this difference. If we continue to look to the past for how to handle the present we will end up with is a self-fulfilling prophecy.

The degree to which the U.S. government took to treating the war in Iraq like Vietnam was clear in the counterinsurgency manual drafted by our military. The manual is full of lessons learned from Vietnam. However, the war in Iraq and the war on terror in general, were not like Vietnam. While it might not always have seemed like it, the Viet Cong and the NVA both had a more defined command structure. That we took out Osama bin Laden and the fighting continues seems to be a pretty good indication of the lack of a centralized command authority. We have been trying to fight terrorism like we would fight a traditional war: employ a decapitation strategy to take out the commanders and then pick the rest of the enemy's military part one piece at a time. This strategy worked great against Saddam Hussein. However, it seems pretty futile against a decentralized fighting force.

The one thing that we as U.S. citizens need to become aware of is that terrorism is not a crime, and it is not an act of war. Terrorism is an unadulterated act of evil. We are not going to negotiate a truce with terrorists. Al Qaida is not a foreign power, and I hesitate to even refer to them as a "transnational terror organizations" as some experts in the field have. It seems more like a loose network of groups who can come together when it benefits them and disperse when the heat is on. The only way for the United States to deal with this threat is to eliminate the cause for which they are threatening us.

We have to learn to fight these types of combatants with a different arsenal of weapons. The best way to stop terrorism is to create a situation where the citizens view the terrorists to be doing more harm then good. We need to find ways to create jobs so the citizens of these nations see something worth living for. Imagine how different the events of September 11th would have been if the citizens of this country didn't believe we had something to live for. In this regard freedom is very much like a material possession. You don't know what it's like to not have a car until you get into a situation where you had one and then lose it. If we can find a way to provide the citizens of at risk nations with good jobs then they can see the opportunities which are worth fighting for. When terror is the only thing you know, it becomes pretty hard to imagine something else.

I'll be honest with you, if the terrorists really wanted to hurt the U.S. they would stop fighting. If the war on terror ended today The United States would be in a world of trouble. We would bring most of our troop's home and begin downsizing our military. Based on the current state of our nation's economy we would have a lot of unemployed veterans of the war. Added to the problems with the housing market and we would end up with a lot of people homeless. Then to top it all off all of the homeless, unemployed people would be left without medical insurance. This nation would be real lucky if we weren't in a civil war ourselves within five years. The terrorists have failed to realize that given enough rope our politicians will hang themselves and the entire nation along with them.

Unfortunately, in a sad ironic twist, the protesters here in the U.S. have failed to notice this as well. A situation which started as a war to combat international terrorism has become a major economic force within our nation. If we were to call all of the troops home right now we would be left with one gigantic mess to clean up. Worst of all is the fact that we will probably end up right back over there after Iran invades Iraq. Iran wouldn't think twice of invading Iraq to get some revenge for the Iran-Iraq War. It seems consistent with the line of thought in Iran to eventually invade Iraq. So Iran seems to have given up its nuclear weapons ambitions for the time being. In reality it makes sense for Iran to give up on nuclear weapons, as they won't need them to invade Iraq and defeat a vastly undermanned military. Iran going after Iraq is something that eventually will take place. Wars in this part of the world are like death and taxes.

I understand there are some people out there who wish we never fought wars, and would like to see our government disband the United States military. I completely support their right to protest against wars, and maybe in some cases those individuals act as a sort of counter balance to the "hawks" in the Department of Defense. But with that said let me retell to the best of my ability a short story. Back in the late 1990's the Discovery Channel aired a documentary about the United States Navy SEALs. Towards the end of the documentary there was an interview with a Master Chief assigned to one of the SEAL teams, and the Master Chief told this story. The U.S. Navy has a process by which they select sailors and Marines to join the SEAL teams. Part of this selection process involves a grueling six day period where the sailors are pushed to their physical and mental breaking point. This six day period is very appropriately referred to as "Hell Week". During one "Hell Week" there was a group of sailors standing at attention on the beach and a drill instructor was standing at the top of a sand dune. The instructor raises his hand to shield his eyes from the sun as he scans the horizon far out to sea, and as he does so he asks the men in front of him if any of them can tell him what he is looking for. No one responds. The instructor continues to scan the horizon, asking again if any of the men can tell him what he is looking for, and again there is no response. Finally the instructor answers his own question. He says "I'm looking to the horizon; I'm looking for the next war."

Since the dawn of civilization human beings have fought wars. Some wars are fought over very bad reasons. Some wars are fought for really good causes. Now I could recite St. Augustine's Theory of Justifiable Warfare and we could debate the meaning of it. However, there are some things about war which are not debatable. People die in wars. The people who get hurt most in wars are often the people who can least bare the cost. But more then anything else, war is inevitable. There will always be someone out in the world looking to cause problems, looking to bully their neighbors, looking to stake claim to some resources for their nation. And like it or not, the United States as the most powerful nation in the world has an obligation to stand up to those bullies and fight for the people who can't fight for themselves. This idea is probably best surmised by the motto of the United States Army Special Forces, De Oppresso Liber, which roughly translates "To Free The Oppressed".

It's clear that in the area of "common defense" (or national security) we have a lot of work to do. Our military must have all of the training and equipment that is necessary for them to provide a proper defense for our nation. We need to work on renewable energy alternative now the same way that we worked on the space program in the 1950s and 60s; this problem cannot be left for the next generation. We must understand our sense of national security requires us to hold individuals and companies accountable for what they do abroad. As a nation we must be willing to bare the cost of liberty and freedom, sending our troops to protect those ideals around the world. It has often been said "freedom is not free" and this statement is more true today then ever before.

THE ART OF FIGHTING TERRORISM

Now in discussing national defense I touched on the issue of fighting terrorism, and seeing as terrorism is one of the biggest threats facing the United States today, feel the need here to dedicate a chapter to this issue and discuss how we as a nation are viewing terrorism worldwide.

As with a lot of other aspects of society, we tend to lump terrorism together into one idea. In reality there are different types of terrorism. There are in fact good reasons for terrorism. Let's face it, our founding fathers where committing an act of terrorism during the Boston Tea Party. French resistance fighters during World War II would have been considered terrorists by the Nazis. Clearly it doesn't seem right to lump terrorist groups such as Hamas, Hezbolla, or Al Qaida into the same group as freedom fighters. Now it could be argued that all of these groups are fighting for freedom in some way. The difference is the "freedom" some of them are fighting for necessitates the oppression of someone else. In order to understand terrorism and fight it, we have to know how it works. Terrorism takes on two very different forms.

Terrorism is a tool, a weapon like any other in an arsenal. The truth be known, terrorism is one of the most effective weapons available. While terrorism does not generally kill as many people as a weapon of mass destruction, it kills and injures more at a far lower cost to the attacker. The lower cost to kill ration is the reason terrorism is so popular in many parts of the world. Terrorism is the result of people fighting with the weapons they have, which is similar to the comment former Secretary of Defense Donald Rumsfeld made some years back regarding the supplying of troops in Iraq. Its part of the nature of warfare, militaries fights with the weapons available and in doing so using the weapons best suited to accomplishing the necessary goal.

Terrorism stands out from other weapons in the real damage done is not by the attack itself but as a result of the residual effect of terrorizing the populace. It's this fear of a future attack that gives terrorism its power as a weapon. People are scared of the unknown, its part of our natural survival instincts. If we know some form of danger is coming towards us we get out of the way. However, with terrorism there is no forewarning in most cases. We can almost perform an autopsy of sorts on any given terrorist attack. The terror group begins by planning out the attack. They gather intelligence on targets. They look at the resources which are available during the attack. Then the terror group picks a team of individuals based on the skills that will be needed. This continues until the attack is finally carried out.

It's interesting to note the method the terrorist organizations go through is very similar to what our own special forces do when planning a mission. If you read about the preparations for Operation Eagle Claw, the failed attempt to rescue U.S. hostages in Iran in the 1980's, and then read the accounts of how the 9/11 attacks came together you will see some of the same principles being used. This is not a coincidence that the two planning situations bare some parallels. The nature of both terrorism and special operations is similar. Their both small scale operations which require a certain amount of concealment until the operation is over and the success of the operation is based in large part on the intelligence that is available during the planning process. Furthermore, both special operations and terrorism are designed to have a psychological effect on the target.

Terrorism is a weapon of war and needs to be treated as such. Would you seriously expect the NYPD to take on the army of the People's Republic of China? The NYPD wouldn't stand a chance in a fight against an army. Local police departments do not have the training, manpower or resources to fight a war. I realize there are some police chiefs out there who would disagree with this assessment. I also realize those same police chiefs and their departments represent a bigger problem than asset in the current situation. There is a world of difference between a drunk who beats up his wife and then barricades himself inside his house and a trained terrorist who will not think twice about shooting a hostage to achieve their operational goals.

For all of the effectiveness of terrorism, it is of little use in a lot of ways. Many terror groups are like Al Qaida, loosely connected groups with a common goal. These types of groups lack the force numbers necessary to achieve their goals against a bigger opponent. Terrorists try to make their fight out to be akin to a David vs. Goliath battle, but in reality it's far from it. David had a weapon that was clearly capable of slaying Goliath. Terrorism is simply not a powerful enough weapon to accomplish this objective, not even when using WMDs. In order for the terrorism to succeed against a government, it must convince the citizens they will be safer without the government in control, and thus the safe bet is to back the terrorists or simply stand on the sidelines while the two sides fight it out.

The need for the support or indifference of the populace represents the major problem facing any terrorist. Terrorism by its very nature attacks the populace. We learned this lesson in Vietnam; it's hard to win over the hearts and minds of the people when those same people are dying in the streets. Sure, terrorism will achieve success in creating a degree of uncertainty among the populace in regards to the government, but its effects are generally short lived and if anything can serve to galvanize a populace behind an existing government. Sustained terrorism has more of an effect, but terrorist often resort to using suicide attacks which diminish their resources rapidly rendering sustainability a problem. After all, there have to be people willing to commit suicide in order for the attack to take place.

Bin Laden made a major strategic mistake when he attacked the United States. The plan Al Qaida conceived expected the United States to attack them in Afghanistan following the 9/11 attacks. Bin Laden believed he would be able to bog the U.S. military down in Afghanistan the same way the mujahadeen had the Soviet Union. However, Bin Laden forgot the mujahadeen had a little help in their fight with the Soviets, namely a lot of weapons and tactical knowledge provided by the United States. Without the assistance which was granted to the mujahadeen by the United States they would have never been able to fend off the Soviet Union. One of the key elements the U.S. provided to the fighters in Afghanistan in the 1980s was intelligence, the same intelligence which is so important to the successful completion of operational goals.

This all goes to demonstrate that the problem with terrorism as a weapon of social change is also the reason terrorism is a weapon of war. Terrorism is only an effective weapon when it is used by a state level power. This is the reason state sponsors of terrorism are viewed to be so dangerous. In most cases it is only with a government sponsoring the terror group that they are able to have any real success. A key example of this can be seen in Hezbollah, a terrorist group that is backed by Iran's Revolutionary Guard. The support Hezbollah receives from Iran allows them to gather resources and recruit new terrorists. In the Middle East Hezbollah functions under the disguise of being a charity organization, they provide food, shelter and education to the public. The problem is this charity comes with a price tag attached; the children who grow up with this charity feel indebted to Hezbollah, and thus are willing to carry out terrorist attacks for them when they become adults.

Al Qaida is very different from Hezbollah and other state sponsored terror groups. Bin Laden's entire plan revolved around getting western powers, particularly the United States, involved in numerous conflicts in the Middle East with the hope of eventually other nations in the region will join together and defeat the west. Up until this point the plan has failed, due in large part to the fact the nations comprising the European Union are looking to negotiation as opposed to aggression in dealing with the Iran. This is in large part due to the serious economic instability in the EU. This is one area where I think President Obama is making some wise moves, but he has to be careful. Unfortunately, President Obama clearly has not gained the trust of the member nation on the European Union to make the strides necessary on this issue. Furthermore, many of the nations in the Middle East are too busy making money off of oil and other trade networks which would be destroyed by a large scale regional conflict. These trade networks are the reason Al Qaida likes to attack oil pipelines in Saudi Arabia and Iraq, in the hopes that by decreasing the flow of oil they can force the respective governments into a conflict with the west. Fortunately, this plan is so flawed it was destined to fail from the beginning.

So what can we learn from all of this? First, terrorism is a weapon of war, closely associated in design and function to special operations in modern militaries. Second, for terrorism to be successfully deployed as a weapon it must be part of a sustained campaign over a period of time in order to achieve the desired psychological effect on the populace. Third, sustaining a terrorist campaign is very difficult, and almost impossible without the aid of a state sponsor. Fourth, as a result of the attacks against the populace, terrorism is much more likely to turn the citizens against the terror group than against the government.

Now that we've looked at terrorism as a weapon of war, let's turn to looking at terrorism as a tool of change. The goal of a terrorist is to make the citizens believe the government is unable to protect them from the actions of the terrorists. This goal is designed to make the public believe they are better off without any government, or better yet the fanatical government the terrorists want to impose, as opposed to the existing government. As stated earlier, the terrorists will gain some small victories in creating a level of uncertainty within the populace. However, if we look at the aftermath of terror attacks across the globe we begin to see an interesting pattern develop.

Terror attacks in industrialized nations are never as successful as those in more under developed countries. Attacks in the United States, the United Kingdom, Spain, Russia and Japan have a completely different result than in Iraq, Pakistan, or Afghanistan. This is not to say the attacks don't kill as many people or do as much damage in industrialized nation, but rather the attacks don't have the same impact on the level of confidence in the government. The explanation for this difference comes to us in the form of Maslow's Hierarchy of Need. People in industrialized nations are generally having these needs met is some way by the government or some other societal actor. The same cannot be said of less developed nations where the most basic of Maslow's needs are not being fulfilled. While the attacks of 9/11 were horrific and saddened the nation and the world, most U.S. citizens still had the essentials needed for life, gainful employment and the hope of better days. However, think of how someone living in Baghdad, Iraq must feel when there is a suicide bombing? On top of not having enough food for their children, a general lack of good medical care, and a high unemployment rate, now they have to deal with some scumbag terrorist trying to kill their family. It takes little for the citizen to jump to the conclusion that if the government can't provide for the most basic of needs, then how will they ever be able to protect the citizens from the terrorists?

Remember the quote from Thomas Paine regarding security I cited in Chapter 2:

> Wherefore, security being the true design and end of government, it unanswerably follows that whatever form thereof appears most likely to ensure it to us, with the least expense and greatest benefit, is preferable to all others.

The terrorists are applying this same idea here for social change. By selecting the form of government being offered by the terrorists the citizens might not have food and shelter and the other necessities of life, but at least they won't be in fear of suicide attacks. The citizens are forced to pick from the less of two evils.

This is where the true power of terrorism lies, with its ability to take citizens who are already feeling beaten down by society and cause them to believe that their lot in life will be better after the terrorists get their way. Thus it is along this line where I believe the ability to defeat terrorism is found. People who have hope are people not given over to the fears of terrorism. So if we wish to win the war on terrorism then we need to find ways to give people hope. I'm not talking about "winning over the hearts and minds" here. I'm talking about giving the citizens of less industrialized nations real jobs. I'm talking about making Iraq and Afghanistan industrialized nations where the citizens have a future. Furthermore, providing these jobs does not mean that we have to take jobs from U.S. citizens. Companies like Ford, General Motors and Proctor and Gamble need to be encouraged to build factories in these nations to provide products for those citizens. There is a risk involved, but it's a risk worth taking. For example, Iraq would be a great candidate for automotive manufacturers, oil pipeline manufacturers, and a host of other consumer products.

Helping to build the economy of the region seems like a simple idea, but it's also one that we as a nation have overlooked. We have lost sight of the fact the United States was successful in becoming a democracy largely because of the existing economic infrastructure which was in place following the Revolutionary War. In the late 18th Century the United States had a thriving lumber industry, ship building trade and other industries which helped to establish the economy of a growing nation. Some of these industries are ones we would rather forget. The slave fueled cotton and tobacco industries of the antebellum south are not a highlight of U.S. history. But as despicable a practice as slavery was, those industries helped to establish the U.S. economy. If we want to see the importance of these industries to our own democracy we need look no further than the impact of the trade embargo imposed during the Jefferson administration as evidence.

There can be little debate that providing a strong foundation to the economic system of newly formed democracies will greatly enhance the possibility of those democracies continuing into the future. A strong economy often leads to a strong society which is much less likely to bend to the will of terrorists. So how do we work to develop these kinds of strong economies in less developed nations? The answer is two fold. First we must get business leaders to develop jobs in these nations. Since it involves a risk there will have to be some kind of economic incentive to get this done, possibly in the form of tax breaks. Secondly, we must keep our military in place until these nations are established. Yes, the U.S. citizens might need to take one on the chin for the rest of the world to make things safe. The moment businesses try to build in Iraq or Afghanistan the terrorists are going to attack the work sites and the effort will be for nothing. However, with the military in place to fight the terrorists it gives businesses the time needed to become established. As it is we use the military simply as a tool to fight terrorism, but in reality we need to use the military as a buffer between society and the terrorists who are wishing to tear society apart.

There is a component of timing when it comes to terrorism, and using the military as a buffer against terrorism is one of the best ways to offset this timing aspect. Ideally the military should not be trying to defeat the terrorists, but rather buy enough time for the society to strengthen itself against the onslaught that is to come. Let there be no doubt a terrorist attack will come, it's virtually inevitable. We as a nation have seen first hand that no matter how sophisticated a nation's intelligence system, some nut job always slips past to commit an attack. The goal here is not to stop every terrorist, but to limit the impact of the terrorists we can't stop so the blow to society will be less when the inevitable occurs.

One of the major problems our nation will face over the years to come as we work to defeat terrorism is the need for a military capable of fighting a new kind of warfare. In some ways we are faced with similar problems to those General Washington faced during the early years of the Revolutionary War. As the war on terror has continued our military has been left with a dwindling number of troops. Furthermore, as the military will admit, the bar has been lowered in order to meet the troop requirements, thus leading to a military made up of troops that some feel are less capable to fight a new type of war. Where we need highly educated troops, we are left, by some accounts, with few high school educated troops and even fewer with college degrees.

What our military and political leadership is failing to realize is the kind of military we have now can be useful, just not for the kind of fighting they envision. Our best bet here is to allow the regular front line military and National Guard units to act as garrison forces and guard the growing infrastructure of the nations where they are deployed. We need to use Special Forces to fight the terrorist, since by its very nature terrorism requires unconventional warfare tactics. Unfortunately, the higher ups in the military command structure are more worried about sending the troops they have under their command into battle so they can add stars to their collars. The work that covert operations carry out rarely ever gain people promotions, as they are covert and no one know the action took place.

While there are some areas where I feel strongly that the government should take a stronger action in, the military is not necessarily one of them. We have some of the best trained military leaders in the world. Would someone please tell me why a president, particularly one with no military experience like President Obama, is trying to dictate how the military runs a war? Ultimately to win the war on terror we need to allow the military to do its job and have the president focus on developing relations with foreign powers and helping to develop economic incentives for businesses to expand into areas terrorists want to target. The best tool we have in the fight against terrorism is empowering people to rise above the level where terrorists want them to be and ensuring freedom is the best weapon at our disposal for achieving this goal.

Unfortunately, we are not seeing the Obama Administration looking to provide serious strength to our foreign relations. As much as they would like to present the appearance of success in the international arena we saw President Obama generally fail to secure the assistance of our allies to ensure the freedom we have fought for in Afghanistan. In fact, since President Obama took office we've seen a backsliding of our efforts in Afghanistan, even to the point of the reestablishment of tyrannical Islamic laws which were in place under the Taliban.

For the fight against terrorism to ever be successful, and our future generations to have any hope of long term peace, we must have leaders who understand the need to combined military force with economic incentives to form a cohesive plan for the development of freedom throughout the world.

"...AND PROMOTE THE GENERAL WELFARE..."

The area of general welfare might be the biggest problem we as a nation will face in the coming decades. If the government cannot manage to ensure some basic essentials for our citizens, how then can we expect the nation to move forward? As President Lincoln put so well, we are "...a government of the people, by the people and for the people...". It seems only logical to conclude that if the people are not being cared for, then the government will suffer as a result. The people and the government are inseparable. The success of one is inevitably tied to the success of the other and vise versa. It is most fitting for The Preamble to the Constitution to begin with the words "We the People...", because we are all linked together on some level through the spirit of democracy. However, the same spirit of democracy dictates we must work together to ensure some of the common necessities all of our citizens need. Unfortunately, our elected officials have failed to come through on this requirement.

All U.S. citizens should have access to the best health care available. The current status of health care in the United States is ridiculous to say the least. Statistics show that we have the most expensive health care in the world. Yet, in comparison to other industrialized nations in the world we rank near the bottom in all of the major fields used as indicators of national health. We need to make some changes in how we deal with health care. While we clearly need some sort of reform in our health care system; we also need to focus on preventive measures from the beginning. We should be giving tax credits to people who join a local health club and workout. We need to do something about cigarettes. How is it that we have laws which ban certain firearms yet a product like cigarettes that we know will kill people is not banned, and is in fact barely regulated at all. The answer to this question is very simple, our politicians in all their wisdom decided that instead of banning cigarettes, they would simply tax them. Taxing cigarettes would be fine if all of the money was going to treat people affected by diseases caused by smoking. Unfortunately the tax dollars generated from tobacco sales are going to fund all kinds of government programs. As a result, if we actually did manage to ban tobacco so it didn't kill millions of our citizens every year, then our government would go bankrupt! What a fine mess our political leaders have gotten us into.

There was a time when hospitals were run by faith based organizations. When this was the case hospitals were not concerned with turning a profit. Instead the hospital was concerned with doing charity. Now, the major hospital networks are publicly traded companies who are more concerned with their bottom line than with helping another human being. All hospitals and health insurance companies should be required to function as a non-profit entity. Looking to turn a profit on someone else's suffering is one of the most despicable things I can think of. Furthermore, the decisions about an individual's health should be between the individual and their doctor. This means the major pharmaceutical companies should be banned from advertising their products to the common citizen. This might seem like a wild idea to the pharmaceutical industry, but how about we let the doctor determine what is wrong with a person and what is the best medication to treat them with. If less money were spent on advertising the latest and greatest wonder drug, then maybe they wouldn't cost so much. Furthermore, we need to ban the pharmaceutical industry from having any unnecessary influence on doctors. There are some doctors who even now are being pressured to only prescribe the latest drug. It might seem crazy, but if you make a good product then doctors will prescribe it and there will be no need for the high pressure sales tactics.

I guess the health industry just doesn't get the fact there are people dying based on their decisions. Or maybe the more appropriate observation is they just don't care. There are simply too many stories of people who find out that they have some terminal disease and then end up being dropped from coverage by there insurance company. How can a government of the people allow this kind of thing to happen to the people? Our politicians seem to have become really adapt at making it look like they are doing something for the good of the people. In the last few decades we've seen a whole lot of legislation passed; FMLA, ADA, and other acts meant to protect citizens. However, the funniest thing always seems to happen; the business community always seems to find the nice little loop-holes in those laws. It doesn't seem to take them too long to find the loop-holes either, not like they really had to look. After all it was the lobbyists hired by corporate America who probably wrote those loop-holes and as a result the corporate lawyers knew exactly where to look.

The health care industry has become the modern equivalent to slavery. In 1775 Thomas Paine said of slavery, "That some desperate wretches should be willing to steal and enslave men by violence and murder for gain, is rather lamentable than strange." Paine's commentary on slavery raises an important question: what is the difference between making money from the pain and suffering of a slave in the fields and making money from the pain and suffering of a person who is sick or injured? From my way of thinking, making money from a sick person is worse. At least the slave had the ability, as limited as it may have been, to rise up against oppression. Let there be no doubt that while the health care industry's propaganda talks about all the good they do, their only real concern is the bottom line. Health insurance companies won't hesitate to deny care to someone who is dying if it will save the company money. Hospitals might be required to treat individuals who lack insurance in emergencies, but they'll be sure to overcharge the same individual for every little item that was used. Of course the hospital wouldn't do this to the insurance company, because they have a contract to only allow for "acceptable charges".

Even then there are some cases where the insurance companies give the doctors the raw end of the deal. A number of years back I had a knee operation that required two orthopedic surgeons. Unfortunately, the insurance company determined only one surgeon was needed so the second surgeon never got paid. To add insult to injury the surgeon who did get paid, got less then 10% of what he billed the insurance company for! The insurance companies are making a bundle of money playing both sides of the game. Unfortunately this is not a simple game. The winners are making a lot of money and the losers are ending up dead in some cases. I don't know about anyone else, but if the insurance companies are looking to kill my fellow citizens, then their looking to pick a fight with me.

Now some states have decided to take action against the health care problem in the United States. There are a number of current proposals to require citizens to have a mandatory coverage policy. Unfortunately, for most of us it's a step in the wrong direction. The most recent example of this can be seen in the Obama Administrations attempt at health care reform. The requirement passed by Congress is similar to the one enacted in the State of Massachusetts, which decreed that anyone who didn't have medical insurance by December 31st 2007 will now face steep tax penalties. Mandatory insurance is not the answer to the health care crisis in the United States. The only thing mandating insurance coverage will promote is the insurance industry to raise rates on policies. I wouldn't be surprised at all to discover the bill in Massachusetts was proposed by a lobbyist for the health insurance industry or by a politician who gets campaign contributions from a medical insurance company. The supporters of mandated coverage try to defend the practice by point to laws which mandate liability insurance for drivers. However, there is a major difference between car insurance and medical insurance. Individuals have a choice between driving their own car and taking mass transit.

As long as you're alive you have no choice about needing healthcare.

The mandated insurance approach makes it look like people who don't have health insurance are somehow selfish. However, nothing could be further from the truth. This reminds me of the same logic that leads to saying a woman "wants" to be raped. The message this sends is that somehow by not having health insurance you're asking to have an illness come upon you. What next, are we going to say an illness is God's revenge for someone not having insurance? I'm all for asking people to be responsible, but let's ask for responsibility in terms which don't place an unfair burden on the public and allow the insurance industry to make a huge profit at the same time. For instance, let's give tax breaks to people who stay health, to people who don't smoke, to people who have health club memberships. Let's provide for routine screenings for various diseases. We need to chance the way we approach health care, transitioning from this slave trade resembling system we have that focuses on profiting from the sick, to a system that promotes being healthy as a way of life.

The worst part about mandate coverage is how it places the insurance industry in the driver's seat. Some politicians are even promoting the idea that by requiring medical insurance coverage that citizens have choices and thus resulting in lower costs. However, nothing could be further from the truth. We need look no further than the itemized statement for an individual's car insurance policy as proof. Looking at my own car insurance premium I see more than half of my premium is made up of liability coverage, and in the last ten years there has never been a liability claim against my policy. However, my comprehensive coverage is much lower and I've made five comprehensive claims (two for vandalism, two for hail and one for a cracked windshield) in the same ten year period. Liability coverage is much more expensive because it is a requirement. This is the economics of supply and demand; if you're required to have the insurance coverage then they can charge more for it. The insurance companies charge less for comprehensive coverage because the claims tend to be smaller and since the coverage is not required by law they need the coverage to cost less so people will choose to carry it. Now the car insurance companies will claim they charge more because the cost of liability claims is much higher, and I

will acknowledge this to be the case to some extent. None the less I'm confident the insurance industry is also taking advantage of the state laws mandating liability coverage and thus allows them to make more money.

The concept behind this idea for mandatory coverage is what's known as "public choice". This is not the first time politicians have offered up a "public choice" option. This same concept has been put forth as an answer to education in the form of school voucher programs and for social security reform in terms of private investment options. These are all part of a larger idea of privatization of government functions. I will talk more about privatization in a later chapter. However, we do need to look at some of the problems with the public choice option for health care. Public choice works great as long as people can make a choice. Under the mandatory coverage plans, what will inevitably happen is a number of medical insurance companies will spring up offering low premiums and little in the way of coverage. These types of companies will offer no coverage for preventive care and little coverage for anything else. However, since lower income citizens will need insurance, they'll be left with no other choice.

We refer to these as public choice, but in reality only the affluent truly get to choose. Note, that members of Congress get access to a coverage plan that none of us can choose.

The end result of these types of public choice mandated medical insurance policies will be an increased cost of medical care being shouldered by the citizens with no perceived effect on the overall state of our nation's health. Lower income citizens are still left without access to preventive care that is critical to keeping them healthy. The cost of medical insurance will go up since the insurance companies are going to claim they are providing coverage to more people and thus have to pay out on more claims. Then to top it all off the insurance industry will do everything possible to take advantage of the situation since the government has shown its inept ability to actually regulate the insurance industry. These policies represent a losing proposition to the U.S. citizens.

In the end mandated health insurance does not resolve the healthcare crisis in our nation. Here rests the real problem with mandated health insurance, and one of the overall problems we face as a nation. For far too long we have seen problems as being mutually exclusive. As I mentioned in the earlier comments about security and liberty, most problems in society are connected to other issues. Healthcare is the same. We have higher healthcare costs because we are an overweight unfit nation. We must make living a healthy life style a priority for any healthcare reforms to succeed.

There is little doubt the hospitals and insurances companies are out to make a profit; and if that means some people die then so be it. Let's take a hypothetical situation. Say a person 30 years of age develops a life threatening heart condition. The condition requires him to quit working. Because he has a known heart condition he can't get regular insurance coverage. Thus this person is left with two choices: one, he goes into debt to get one of the new government high risk plans, begin treatment and eventually declares bankruptcy, or he doesn't get treated and ends up dying. It would seem the first choice is the best one, but not so fast. After he gets treated and recovers and declares bankruptcy he'll go looking for a job and he won't be able to find one because of a bad credit score. So now he's out of work, unemployable, unable to afford the medication to treat his heart condition, and living under a bridge where the heart condition finally kills him after all. The result is the same; it just took longer to get there. The sad fact is these kinds of scenarios do play out in this country today, and the reason these scenarios occur is because of one word: greed. I'm all for capitalism, but I draw the line at using capitalism as the justification for issuing a death sentence to another human being.

There are solutions for the health care crisis. I propose in addition to requiring hospitals and medical insurance companies to be non-profit entities we open the medical insurance system that is available to federal employees to all citizens. Now the medical insurance would not be offered free of charge. Rather we would require individuals to work a certain number of hours of civil service to offset the cost. There are all kinds of jobs which need to be done in the federal government and for various non-profit groups which would more than help to divert the cost of providing medical insurance. We can have people training as first responders in case of emergencies. We can have people working to provide child care for single parents who wish to attend college classes to further their careers. We can have people doing routine paper work as opposed to paying a federal law enforcement agent to do it. Citizens could spend Saturdays delivering the mail so that postal employees can have the day off. This would prove to be a great opportunity for individuals who work part-time jobs that have no health benefits. This plan would benefit college students who in addition to getting medical insurance would also get valuable work experience. Best of all it would get a lot of citizens more involved with their government. This is a win-win situation, and yet I've not heard a proposal like this from our current political leadership. This is not a foreign concept. It's actually the same sweat equity concept used by Habitat for Humanity, just applied to a different area of society.

The citizens should know they will be taken care of in the event of a natural disaster. This function of the government exists in two parts. First, the government needs to make sure all citizens are safe before, during and immediately after a disaster takes place. We saw how the government failed to provide for this in New Orleans. My vision is for every U.S. citizen to be issued a new social security card that doubles as a debit card. Each card would be inactive, have $2,000.00 on it, and the cards would be distributed based on zip codes. In the event of an emergency the president could issue an order to activate all of the cards in the affected zip codes. As a result people would have the money they need to evacuate, find shelter and pay for food until the appropriate federal and state organizations arrive to render aid. Secondly, after the disaster is over, the government needs to provide what ever aid is needed to rebuild. We know disasters like tornados, floods, hurricanes and wildfires take place in this country every year; so why are we not prepared for what we know to be inevitable.

Of course the good old insurance companies will help us. If you believe your insurance company will help you I have some ocean front property just outside Denver I'd like to sell you. Once again, just like health care, insurance companies are only looking out for themselves. If your house gets destroyed, you better have a good lawyer because you're going to need one. If your car gets totaled in an accident, you can forget about getting a fair price. The insurance companies and the finance industry have created a nice little racket. See they have this little "black book" of prices that none of the rest of us can see. Funny thing, the price listed in the "black book" is never the same as the price of the same vehicle at a dealership. Thus, when your car gets totaled the amount the insurance company is willing to pay you is always lower than the replacement cost of the vehicle. The end result is you have to finance part of the vehicle you buy to replace the vehicle which was totaled.

Now I'm going to cut the insurance industry off at the pass on this one. See, the insurance industry tries to argue that they are only responsible for the market value of the car and not the replacement value. Now I completely agree the insurance company should not responsible for buying a brand new car to replace a car which is five years old. However, when you find a vehicle the same make, model, year, and with similar mileage we're not talking about replacement cost but rather the going market rate for a particular vehicle. However, that's not the way the insurance industry sees it, and since you really have no means of arguing with them, outside of going to court or talking to a useless state insurance commissioner, you're stuck with their decision in collusion with others in the industry. Why can't our government put an end to this kind of unethical activity on the part of the insurance industry? But after all, with all the money the politicians are getting from the insurance lobbyists, why would they want to stop unethical activity?

The events which take place following a natural disaster represent the best test of the capabilities of a government to provide for the citizens. In the wake of a disaster citizens look to the government for the bare essentials needed to survive, food, water and shelter. The government has become lax in providing for these needs after a disaster, leaving the matter to the American Red Cross. In May of 2007 former President Bush finally signed a bill to fix some of the problems which persisted with the American Red Cross. I'm all for the U.S. government looking to non-profit groups for help in the wake of a disaster, but the government should still be the group most concerned with the welfare of citizens. However, it seems the government is more concerned with spinning the story for the media and leaving groups like the American Red Cross to help people.

As stated before, we know these kinds of disasters will occur, so there is no reason for our nation not to be prepared. We know the areas where these disasters can take place, so why do we not have food and water stock piled in those regions. MREs (Meals Ready to Eat) have a seven year shelf life, so if we haven't used them after six years we give the MREs to local soup kitchens to feed the homeless and re-supply the emergency reserves. Better yet, buy 20% of the food and water a region needs every year incase of a disaster. After the fifth year you're replacing 20% each year as a result every year you have food to give to the homeless. This is a truly win-win situation, if we need the food its there, if we don't the homeless and needy get nutritious meals. Sure, it cost some money, but at the price the U.S. government pays for MREs which are already being produced for the military, the cost per capita would be minimal and we as a nation would have peace of mind knowing the provisions were there if needed.

Every year the U.S. government sells bulk lots of tents and other military surplus at auctions. Why are we not putting these tents into storage incase we need them as shelters after a disaster? Sure, these tents aren't the latest, greatest technology, and these tents won't stand up to weather at Mt. Everest Advanced Base Camp. However, they don't have to; they only need to provide a temporary roof over a family's head until something better can be found. There are a lot of other uses, surplus clothing could be provided after a disaster, there are medical instruments that are sold as surplus which could be used in an emergency. No, none of this is the latest technology, but when it's surplus equipment or nothing, I'd rather have the surplus equipment.

Some of these problems with emergency preparedness are at the local level. I live in Kansas, and we all know in the spring and summer Kansas is practically ground zero for tornado activity. Yet, even to this day cities and counties in Kansas and all across the plains continue to build fire stations above ground. Now, wouldn't it just make sense to build fire stations so the part of the structure which houses the fire fighting apparatus is under ground where a tornado can't damage it? It just makes sense to put the tools you'll need after a disaster, such as fire trucks and ambulances, where they will be accessible after the disaster. After all, an ambulance under a pile of rubble doesn't help injured citizens. We have to begin taking care of the environment a lot better than we currently are. This does not mean we need to engage in fear mongering and lying about the problem. We should be encouraging people to recycle; instead we have cities that charge people to take part in recycling. How does our government expect people to engage in environmental stewardship if the cost of doing so is prohibitive? We need to find ways to make green building more cost efficient. There are some subsidy programs out there but they are not widely used mainly because the general public doesn't know they exist. You regularly see commercials for the latest gas guzzling car or truck, but when was the last time you saw a commercial advertising the benefits of putting solar panels on the roof of your house?

I really don't understand how it is that Christians don't come to take a stand on the side of environmental protection. God says in the Bible "the earth is my footstool", so I have to ask, how would you feel if someone was defecating all over your footstool? Unfortunately solving environmental problems will never occur until we remove the issue of environmental protection from the quagmire of politics. As long as the issue of protecting our environment is championed by politicians then there will be people who see it as being bad. Here we are back at the whole trust issue again. If I can't trust politicians to take care of our government responsibly, then what makes them think I trust them to take care of the environment? We're talking about idiots who actually believe the internet is a group of interconnecting tubes created by Al Gore! What in the world can politicians know about the environment? They know how to get rich off the destruction of the environment by allowing companies to selling carbon credits. This seems like we're going down the same road of bad ideas we went down when we started taxing tobacco. If we allow the sale of carbon credits to take place then our nation will eventually get to the point where some companies will be so dependent on the sale of carbon credits it won't be economically viable to actually do something to protect the environment. Selling carbon credits is a really bad idea. When you are making a profit from negative activities like pollution; then you inevitably end up supporting the negative activity whether you intend to or not.

We need to find ways to encourage the use of mass transit systems. I'll be the first to say there are some cases where mass transit as we know it simply is not an option. Mass transit works great in cities like New York, Chicago and Boston, but in cities that don't have an existing transit system the environmental and financial costs of establishing the system is exceedingly high. Cities on the east and west coasts have always dealt with the fact that space is at a premium. As a result cities in these areas have grown vertically, where cities in the plains, such as Dallas, Oklahoma City and Kansas City, don't have the same issue with space and consequently they have grown horizontally. Mass transit is not a realistic solution for cities which have grown horizontally. Many of the cities in the central part of the country have smaller populations, yet cover more square miles of area in comparison to cities on either coast. As a result establishing a major public transit system in these horizontally established cities will cost more per person. The only answer for these areas is more fuel efficient vehicles.

Once again, we knew years ago there was an energy crisis looming, and yet we did nothing. The automotive manufactures have done very little to create more fuel efficient designs until recently. It wasn't until the last five years when the problem began to hit Detroit in the pocket book that the decision was made to take action in researching new fuel sources. This is not to say SUVs don't have their place. I own a Jeep Grand Cherokee. I also spend a fair amount of time camping, fishing and mountain biking, and unlike the soccer mom, my Jeep sees dirt and I use my four-wheel drive. The soccer mom is simply helping to destroy the earth in order to have a status symbol.

Environmental stewardship is a partnership between the government, the people and the business community. No one group has the ability to make the changes necessary to help resolve the problem. As a nation we have a responsibility not only to the future generations of U.S. citizens, but to our neighbors around the globe, to take the first major steps towards resolving the environmental crisis at hand. The fact is most of the devices which create pollution were invented by our citizens. It was a U.S. citizen, Henry Ford, who developed a mass production method for the automotive industry. As a result of mass production there was an increased need for petroleum based fuels and lubricants, rubber, metals, and all the other elements which go into making a car and keeping it running. We all had a hand in creating this problem and now it only makes sense for us as a nation to bare the responsibility for finding a solution.

In order for the United States to have any kind of future we must ensure our children start off with a quality education in the safest environment possible. This means we protect children from bullies and harassment when they are at school. If we are going to be committed to fighting terrorism overseas, then we need to be committed to fighting it in the school yards as well. We cannot expect children to learn and perform in academic endeavors if they are in fear for their safety. We have to teach that there are consequences for ones actions in society. If a student wants to act out and create a dangerous situation for other students, then the disruptive student needs to be removed from the school. We cannot allow one student to create a problem for the entire population of a school.

We also need to end some of the unfunded mandates the U.S. government has placed on our public school system. Similar to the situation we find with health care, the decisions about the education of our nation's children needs to be made between the educators and the parents. When I say the parents, I mean all the parents, not just the narcissistic soccer mom who wants to run the PTA with an iron fist. Chances are the soccer mom's kid is the one bullying all the other kids in school; I wonder where they learned it from. We need to make sure our children are schooled in the basics so they have a legitimate chance of succeeding in college and the rest of their lives. As it is our public schools are little more than glorified babysitting services as is evident in our nations test scores as they relate to other nations of the world. The best gift we can give our children is a high quality education. Once again this is the idea of laying a foundation and building on it. Future generations must have the knowledge necessary to help the nation grow.

As it is some of our political "leaders" don't even believe in our colleges and universities. There are a number of political pundits, President Obama included, who don't believe our universities are good enough to train future leaders to run our government. Instead, they believe we need to create some form of national service academy to train leaders. I have to admit I find this line of thought to be some what offensive. We have a number of very good universities which have excellent programs training individuals in public policy and public administration. And as a graduate of one of those schools I'm trying to understand why politicians want a new school specifically designed for a function which is already being fulfilled. My initial suspicion is the politicians want to train future public servants to be political puppets. Currently civil servants are trained to do what is in the best interest of the public at large. However, we all know that what's in the public's best interest and what's in a politician's best interest is not always the same.

Currently we have a number of prominent service academies in our nation. Institutions like West Point provide excellent training for our military leaders. However, running the military and running the government is two very different issues. The most disturbing part of a national civil service academy, is having students selected for admission based on similar criteria to what is used for the military academies. This would quite possibly include the requirement of the applying student being nominated by a member of Congress as is the case with the military academies. These nominations are generally not a problem in the military, due in large part to the military chain of command existing independent of Congress. For example, a member of Congress generally can't give orders to second lieutenant fresh out of West Point.

The situation which would exist in the case of a national civil service academy under this same nomination system would be far different. The civilian administrative officials of the federal departments are responsible to members of Congress to provide various reports, information and testimony about the government activities their departments are involved in. While the process of nominating someone from a military academy has little to do with politics, the nomination of individuals to a civil service academy would have massive political implications. I can foresee ethical issues and corruption as the end result. What is there to keep a graduate of a civil service academy from lying to Congress or falsifying some numbers on a report to help the Congressional member who nominated them to get a bill passed?

The jobs civil servants do are hard enough as it is. These are professionally trained, unelected individuals who are doing their best to provide the services the public needs. The notion of some politicians wishing to places them in a compromising position for the benefit of their political power is ridicules. While it's impossible to be completely removed from the effects of politics in the job, civil servants try their best to remain objective in their work. To allow for the formation of a national civil service academy similar to the military academies would do nothing more than set civil service in the United States back over 100 years. We would be returning to the days of political bosses, nepotism, and political favoritism. We as citizens of the United States deserve far better from our government.

It's clear there are serious problems in how the government is providing for the needs of our nation's citizens. We can't expect politicians who use these problems as campaign fodder in order to get elected to be the same people who solve the problems. I doubt there is a citizen in the United States who hasn't listened to a political speech and known the promises the candidate made were as empty as the candidate's moral compass. It is necessary for the citizens of this nation to take up the cause of our own freedom and ensure it is maintained. I firmly believe the future of our nation rests on the ability of the government to protect some of these basic needs. We need to ensure quality healthcare and education to all citizens. How can we expect anyone to achieve their full potential if they are uneducated or sick? We have to stop Corporate America from making a profit by holding people down. All U.S. citizens should have the opportunity to make the best life they can, and for some greedy individual to put road blocks in a citizen's path is unacceptable. Now by no means do I believe we should be giving hand outs to people who don't want to put in the effort to make something of them selves. On the other hand there is no excuse for companies who want to hold hard working citizens down. There is a happy middle ground here; it's just one where big business potentially doesn't make as much money. However, believe it or not, curtailing some of the private sectors greed would probably help save some businesses.

We need to ensure our nation has the best leadership, elected or not, that's available. To do so we must eliminate the use of nepotism in any form and require government officials to hire people who are best for the job at hand and not best for their political aspirations. As a nation we must never forget the citizens come first in our government, and it's time to reaffirm this ideal.

"...AND SECURE THE BLESSINGS OF LIBERTY TO OURSELVES AND OUR POSTERITY..."

Maintaining the freedoms that have been acquired by and protected through the suffering of our fellow citizens is the responsibility of ever single person who claims citizenship in the United States of America. We as citizens of the United States are indebted to those who came before us and created this great nation. It is our duty as citizens to honor their memories by continuing the work they started. Furthermore we have an obligation to the generations to come after us to provide them with the ground work they need to further the success of this nation. In First Corinthians Chapter Three the apostle Paul provides us with a guide to how we should build a church, he says:

According to the grace of God which was given me, as a wise master builder I have laid the foundation, and another builds on it. But let each one take heed how he builds on it.

For no other foundation can anyone lay than that which is laid, which is in Jesus Christ. Now if anyone builds on this foundation with gold, silver, precious stones, wood, hay, straw, each one's work will become clear; for the Day will declare it, because it will be revealed by fire; and the fire will test each one's work, of what sort it is.

Regardless of your religious beliefs, these words ring true of a democracy also. The foundation of democracy laid by our forefathers is the foundation we have, we cannot lay it anew. The generations which followed them built on that foundation by freeing our fellow country men from the bondage of slavery, they insured all citizens have the right to vote, and they went abroad to defend our shores when the vanguards of evil rose up against our way of life. This is not to say everything done by previous generations was right. For example, the forced removal of Native Americans was wrong. We try to make amends for those wrongs while moving the nation forward. As a people we don't have the luxury of going back in time and fixing mistakes. The best we can do is to learn from those mistakes and apply those lessons to decisions we make in the future and hope those future decisions will be right.

It's interesting to note the very different tone President Obama took when discussing the foundation of our nation during his April 29th 2009 press conference to celebrate his firs 100 days as president. President Obama speaks of a "new foundation". Here I am talking about using the foundation of the "city on the hill" to help rebuild this great nation so we can return to prominence, and President Obama is talking of building a new foundation. Maybe it's just me, but if I tear down a house and build it with a new foundation, then in reality I'm building a completely new house. Unfortunately, this is the exact "change" President Obama and the rest of the politicians in Washington D.C. are interested in. Their goal is to change the form of government we have, to change what it means to be a citizen of The United States of America.

Clearly there is a problem; the government has failed to live up to its end of the bargain when it comes to providing for the nation. Let's face it, the Constitution is the original Contract with America, and a pretty good argument has been made that the government is in breach of contract. The question we as citizens need to ask is what do we do about this problem?

In the early days of the Massachusetts Bay colony, the famed Puritan orator Jonathan Winthrop delivered his famous "Model of Christian Charity" sermon. It was in this sermon that Winthrop talked of the future United States as a "shining city on the hill". While I don't believe in everything Winthrop said, I do truly believe in this "city on the hill" principal. The United States is the most powerful democracy in the world today and as such we have a responsibility to provide a good example to the rest of the world. From a distance this city might look good, but close up it's a much different story. In reality the windows are broken, the buildings need a coat of paint and the grass needs to be mowed. Obviously, none of these things are impossible to fix, but they will take some time and effort.

We have to learn that war and violence are not how you grant people freedom. We need to support freedom through economic incentives and other forms of diplomacy. In short we need to follow the idea of spreading freedom with the plow and defending freedom with the sword. Furthermore, people in other nations must decide they want freedom and then fight for it themselves. Once they begin to fight then I have no doubt we should provide them with what support we can, but they must take those first "baby steps" towards being free. The best way to promote democracy and freedom is to show everyone the good that can come from it. Libya has become the perfect example of this idea.

The spirit of democracy is a chain with each generation forming a new link. The question we need to ask ourselves is do we want to look back some years from now and realize we created a broke link? Are we leaving the next generation all the tools they need to continue the work of democracy? And just as Paul states, the work we do will be tested. There will be other events like September 11th. There will be natural disasters which will leave our nation in a sense of shock. What we have to understand is the way future generations will face those issues will be the result of the work previous generations, the current ones included, did to provide the tools necessary to resolve the problems. These tools take on a lot of different appearances and range from basics like education to the more intricate aspects of government. But regardless of the appearance the tools must be there in order for them to be used.

This means we have an obligation to ensure the tools are there to begin with. We need to begin to fulfill these objectives by making politics an even playing field. When I say even the playing field I don't mean in terms of elections between politicians. Rather we need to require politicians to be honest when running for office. How can we as citizens be expected to elect the right candidate if we are forced to sort through the lies we are feed in campaign ads to find the truth. Some of these politicians do nothing more than tell out right lies in their campaign ads. Every campaign season we are inundated with the same bunch of lies as before. The lies seem to take on two different forms.

First are the lies about what the candidate will do if they get elected. It never fails that candidates make promises they have no intention of keeping, but furthermore they lack the political power to make good on to begin with. These are the candidates who promise reforms to the tax code, to cut taxes, institute social security reforms, and so forth. Seeing how it requires a majority vote in Congress to succeed at any change, and we have a general lack of leadership in Congress, it seems highly unlikely for a single person will make difference in Congress, or even want to.

The second type of lie is just as destructive, but often involves candidates who are seeking re-election. These are the cases where a candidate lies about the work they've done in the past. Let me provide a good example of this. In 2006 while running for re-election, former Kansas governor Kathleen Sebellius ran a series of campaign ads where she claimed to be responsible for the increase in school funding in the State of Kansas. The truth however, was far different from what the ads presented to the voters. In reality it was the Kansas Supreme Court who ordered the State Legislature to reconvene in special session to deal with the issue of school funding or face contempt charges if they didn't comply. Governor Sebellius was only involved in signing the bill into law. If that lie wasn't enough, Governor Sebellius further claimed in ads that during her term in office taxes went down for Kansas residents. While this is true, it would be more accurate to say Governor Sebellius wanted to raise taxes and was only stopped by the State Legislature. This is who President Obama wants to guide our nation in the fight against potential pandemics? Ask the citizen's of Greensburg, Kansas and Coffeyville, Kansas how well she did taking care of them.

I personally find this second type of lie to be more disgusting, because the intention is to make the voter believe the candidate has been doing a good job when often nothing could be further from the truth. These ads are developed by political spin doctors like Karl Rove and James Carvalle. The modern theory of politics seems to hold that the truth has as many incarnations as the human mind can conceive. Politicians have taken to looking at the truth as some abstract idea, where their truth and someone else's truth are not always the same. There are a lot of things in life that are relative only to themselves. Time and culture among other things are relative unto themselves. However, there is a point where the truth is the truth and a lie is a lie.

Allowing politicians to actively engage in this type of activity when it comes to political campaigns is dangerous to the democratic process. After a while it begins to undermine the trust of the voters. The lack of trust, resulting from the lies our politicians have told us is one of the reasons voter turn out tends to be so low over the last few decades. Why should anyone vote? We don't know who we're really voting for; all we can do is vote for who ever supplies the best sounding pack of lies. All the candidates are telling the voters what they think we want to hear. They use polls and surveys to collect data on which lie they should tell.

If we want to return control of our nation to the citizens, then we need to take action to ensure the voters have all of the information needed to make an informed decision in the

72

polling booth. Lying to the voters in a campaign should be treated as the serious offense it is. From the point of maintaining the legitimacy of the elected government, it is detrimental to allow politicians to continue telling lies as a means of getting elected. As citizens in a democracy it is our responsibility to take a firm stand on issues such as dishonest and corrupt politicians. I propose we pass a law making it a criminal offense to knowingly lie during a political campaign. There are two important reasons why this should be dealt with as a criminal matter. First, the severity of the action and the ability to undermine the democratic process dictates a crime has occurred. Secondly, the determination should be made by the public acting through a jury and due process of law to determine if the crime has been committed.

It's bad enough the politicians are lying, but it would be even worse if we were to allow the politicians to deal with the matter themselves through congressional powers or administrative function. Allowing Congress to deal with the matter would result in politicians being censured and the use of the law as a political weapon by the opposing party. The last thing we need is a law designed to ensure trust in the democratic process being used for the motives of political parties and degrade the trust further.

The penalties for lying to the voters should be tough and representative of the severity of the offense. If a politician is found guilty of lying there should be three penalties enforced. First, the politician should be removed from any elected office or government position they are holding at the time. Secondly, they should face a $50,000 fine to help pay for the cost of prosecuting their case. And third, the politician should be barred from running for elected office for a period of ten years following the first offense and for life following a second offense.

As it stands I question whether we as citizens are really making a choice when it comes to elections. Some years ago I was having a discussion about elections in a class I was take, and I came up with an analogy for elections. Imagine that someone tells you they are either going to punch you in the face or kick you in the face, but you get to decide which one it will be. Are you really being given a choice? Your nose is going to be broken both ways and you're going to end up in the emergency room of the local hospital. That's not much of a choice.

We have a major issue with members of Congress using their power for their own gains. Let's take for example the situation surrounding the Major League Baseball steroid scandal. The House of Representatives' Committee on Oversight and Government Reform had no business holding hearings on this issue. While these hearings were occurring we continued to be threatened by terrorists around the globe who want to destroy our way of life, deal with a border as porous as a sponge, a health care system that's completely inefficient, and an education system that is failing our children. Furthermore, while Congress was talking about steroids we had a crisis breaking out on Wall Street which left our nation's economy at the brink of disaster. However, instead of instead dealing with those or any other important issues, Congress choose to deal with the steroids scandal. I guess some members of Congress lost a little too much money betting on the World Series.

The Chairman of the House of Representatives' Committee on Oversight and Government Reform at the time was Rep.

Henry Waxman, who was elected by the voters of California's Tenth Congressional District. A lot of voters in the United States, me included, saw a glimmer of hope on the horizon a few years back when the citizens of California took a monumental step forward and recalled an ineffective governor. I for one thought we were going to see the citizens of this great nation take back control of our government and begin to set in motion the reforms which are so desperately needed. Unfortunately it appears we were all wrong.

No, instead the citizen of the United States were forced to watch as Rep. Waxman and his cronies wasted tax dollars on some frivolous hearings all for the purpose of generating free publicity for their re-election campaigns. The tax dollars spent on those hearings could fund research into a cure for cancer, provide prenatal care to low income mothers, provide more police officers to make our streets safe, and a lot of other important functions the government is tasked with providing to the citizens. In fact, I've been through the United States Constitution backwards and forwards and have yet to find the section that provides the federal government the power to regulate Major League Baseball or any other professional sports for that matter. I guess this is simply another example of the powers Congress has appointed unto itself without the consent of the U.S. citizens.

If a crime has been committed then allow the appropriate government agency to deal with the matter. I seriously doubt these hearings will lead to any new laws designed to help make the citizens safer. Wouldn't it be a lot wiser to use the money which was spent on those hearings and put it towards programs to educate junior high and high school athletes about the dangers of using performance enhancing substances?

I decided to discuss the Congressional investigation into the use of performance enhancing drug intentionally when closing this chapter for a reason. The investigation illustrates the real problem we face with our elected officials today, not their inability to act on issues but their unwillingness to act unless they have something to gain by doing so. We as a nation have seen problems coming for years in advance yet our elected officials continue to ignore the problems. How can we expect to "bestow the blessings of liberty" if our government refuses to stop the degradation of our rights and ideals until it's too late? How can we be expected to trust our own government when our government sends a signal indicating they don't care about the problems we face? It seems to me the only way Congress is willing to deal with any problem is when they are left with no other choice. Once the banks started to collapse, the stock market took a nose dive and members of Congress and their wealthy friends started losing piles of money, only then did the issue of our dire economic situation take on a sense of urgency. Only when the issue creates problems for a politician's pocket book or their chance to get reelected does it begin to matter. The sad part is, our enemies have realized this too. Have you ever noticed how terrorist attacks rarely take place during election years? My question to my fellow citizens is; when do we start to take responsibility for fixing some of these problems ourselves?

PROBLEMS TOO NUMEROUS,
SOLUTIONS TOO FEW

In the Declaration of Independence Thomas Jefferson wrote the following:

> Prudence, indeed, will dictate that governments long established should not be changed for light and transient causes; and accordingly all experience hath shown that mankind are more disposed to suffer while evils are sufferable, than to right themselves by abolishing the forms to which they are   accustomed. But when a long train of abuses and usurpations, pursuing invariably the same object, evinces a design to reduce them under absolute despotism, it is their right, it is their duty to throw off such government, and to provide new guards for their future security.

We are not dealing with "...light or transient causes...", rather we are dealing with issues that will determine the future of this great nation. We as a nation must find new ways of constructing our government to hold it more accountable to the citizens. Let me be very clear here that I am in no way calling for any kind of armed revolt; rather I am calling on the citizens of the United States to take a political stand for what is right in the hope that such bloodshed can be avoided in the future. Earlier I spoke of the spirit of democracy as a chain with each generation forming a new link. Democracy cannot support itself indefinitely without the people helping. Once again we are back to the idea mentioned earlier that the nation and the individual are linked together in this system of government. This concept of the "haves" and the "have nots" cannot continue and be of any benefit to the nation as a whole. Class warfare is not of benefit to our nation. If anything this concept will be the ruin of the nation in that the upper class will in all likelihood continue their attack on the middle class until the gulf between the rich and the poor is so vast it cannot be bridged. It is at that point we end up with a very bloody and protracted civil war. And I assure you the results coming out of the war will be nothing like what our forefathers envisioned for this nation.

We as a nation must reclaim our country from the corrupt politicians, high powered lobbyists and corporations. And I have to reiterate here violence is not the answer, rather we as a people need to come together as one nation with a common goal of pursuing a better future for all citizens. When problems arise now we have a tendency to not deal with the problem as a nation but as individual groups within the nation. "We the people" make up the United States of America. No one group should be able to arbitrarily make decision about the future of this nation; no group within this country is a nation unto itself. It's almost as if there is a chain link fence in front of us collectively. Through this fence we can see the promise land; we can see the land Dr. King described in his dream. However, we can't seem to understand that pervious generations have made sacrifices to acquire the land for us. All we have to do is stop living in the past, break down the fence and take possession of our rightful inheritance.

Simply stated there are some people who are making money by forcing us to live in the past. The entertainment industry is one of the biggest contributors to this problem. What was the last major blockbuster movie where the problems of the protagonist were solved through dialogue? While these movies do exist they are few and far between. In all likelihood the first thing a character in a movie is going to do when faced with a problem is reach for a gun. Violence, and by extension warfare, are options of last resort, they should never be the first choice.

Thanks to an inappropriate comment by Don Imus made a few years ago, the issue of music came into the public spotlight. Slavery ended over 140 years ago, yet there are hip-hop artists today who see women the same way plantation masters saw female slaves in the antebellum south. It is degrading to treat women as property. Some country music does its best to make being an uneducated alcoholic seem cool, and some rock music glamorizes drug use.

The entertainment industry needs to begin holding itself accountable for the message it sends to our nation. How can we be expected to thrive as a nation if the message being sent is one of using drugs, being drunk, and abusing women? It's time for the entertainers to do their part for bettering this nation and stop sabotaging the future. Entertainment needs to

79

be projecting the best and worst of what our society has to offer, not just the worst.

This is not to say I am in any way promoting censorship. Rather I am saying parents need to be more aware of the influences their children are exposed to. Entertainment, whether it is music, film, literature, or some other media, is a form of artistic expression. The problem is that while art is meant in some cases to imitate life, the art of entertainment is not imitating life so much as it is defining life. For example, I can see a certain place for violence in some films, but if violence were as common as movies make it seem we would be a nation of 100 million instead of 300 million. If prostitution and drug and alcohol abuse were as rampant as some music makes it seem we would get nothing done and a lot more people would have AIDS. As a nation we need to make sure our buying habits are inline with who we are as a nation and not in line with whom marketing people want us to be. Who we are and the people the marketing firms want us to be are rarely the same. While degrading women and using violence to solve problems might have been the standard over 100 years ago, we've come a long way since those days, and its time we start acting in a way that is conducive with these more enlightened ideals.

We must establish for ourselves a national identity that includes all citizens. For far too long individual citizens have been trying to identify with sub-sections of society instead of connecting with society as a whole. This is the desire of politicians and marketing analysts. This allows politicians to focus their campaigns around one or two hot button issues and avoid the aforementioned areas where the government has failed the citizens. Marketing analysts are looking to target specific demographics so they can sell more of some product you probably don't need. Was Dr. King thinking of demographics when he said:

> Let freedom ring. And when this happens, and when we allow freedom ring—when we let it ring from every village and every hamlet, from every state and every city, we will be able to speed up that day when all of God's children—
> black men and white men, Jews and Gentiles, Protestants and Catholics—will be able to join hands and sing in the words of the old Negro spiritual: "Free at last! Free at last! Thank God Almighty, we are free at last.

I seriously doubt Dr King was thinking of marketing or politics.

The government of the United States has been failing for some time now. We've all been taught the normal way for a democracy to function is through the use of a three branch system of government that provides for checks and balances to prevent any one branch from becoming too powerful. The problem is the check and balance system was never intended to be a continual part of a democracy. The system of checks and balances was designed as a fail safe measure. Think of it in terms of this analogy: would you give a loaded hand gun to a five year old child and then watch him closely to make sure the child did not harm himself or someone else? Of course you wouldn't give the kid a gun! It would be much easier to just not give him the gun and there by alleviate the need to keep a close eye on him. The same applies with checks and balances. What intelligent person would willingly give powers to a government you know need to be checked unless it were absolutely necessary?

Earlier I talked of the need for security and how we had to walk a thin line in regards to balancing security with liberty. The check and balance system provides us with the answer. The intent is we only give the government those powers which are absolutely necessary for security and then trust in the fail safes provided through the checks and balance system to ensure the powers are not misused. This system works if the government has not destoyed the trust of the people.

In 1858 Abraham Lincoln made a famous speech when he accepted the Republican senate nomination for the State of Illinois. During this speech Lincoln came out against slavery and referred to the United States as a "house divided". As a nation we are still very much divided. We see politicians using race and gender as dividing points during political campaigns. For all the hard work which has been done in civil rights, there is still a long ways to go.

Unfortunately there are still individuals and groups within our nation who want to create division. Our politicians have learned to thrive on driving a wedge between races, religions, genders, and ethnicities. It all began in the late 60s and early 70s when candidates campaigned in the south based on their stance on civil rights. Unfortunately this trend now has come to divide the nation politically. Worst of all there are individuals who use their status within society to further drive the wedge between our citizens based on race. How can we expect to overcome the disgusting phenomenon that is discrimination as long as there are people making money off of it?

We as a society must learn new ways to cope with the differences inherent to individuals. The ways we have dealt with the problem act only to highlight where we have unfortunately gone wrong in dealing with equality in general. If we can see in grade school students that differences are often pointed out for ridicule and discrimination, then wouldn't it seem that trying to further differentiate groups of people through "diversity" is only going to make the problem worse? I know there are some people out there who will vehemently assail me for saying this, but the fact is diversity breeds discrimination. This is the exact opposite way from how we should be treating the problem. When I walk down a street I don't see an African American person, an Asian American person, a Latin American person or even a Native American person, I see my fellow United States citizens. Why are we trying to emphasis the differences when we have so much in common? I will say this again, diversity breeds discrimination. In order to have diversity you must first segregate people into different groups. You cannot have forced diversity without first discriminating against people. We need to learn to embrace all aspects of our culture equally. In many ways the concept of diversity has created a bigger problem today then was present before. Before diversity was introduced discrimination was easier to spot. It use to be if a company avoided hiring people based on race, gender or some other factor it was obvious. Now, companies hire token members of various groups but still engage in discrimination within the company. Diversity has provided these companies with an easy way to escape ridicule. Discrimination is as rampant in Corporate America today as ever, they've simply been provided with a means of hiding these activities.

Ending discrimination is the one area where the entire nation should come together and develop a solution once and for all. I do my best no to brow beat people with the Bible, but this is one case where I will make an exception. In Acts 17:26 the apostle Paul is preaching the gospel to the citizens of Athens and says "[a]nd He has made from one blood every nation of men to dwell on all the face of the earth…". My belief in Jesus Christ dictates that I treat all people the same, God made all of us from the same basic material. Unfortunately there are some citizens of this nation who see things differently, and I am firmly of the opinion those same people need to leave this nation.

Now I am fully aware that some individuals are going to complain about my use of religion in fighting for equality for all people. I generally try my best to be respectful of others and their beliefs, or lack there of as the case may be. However, equality is the one issue where I will draw the proverbial line in the sand. The abolitionist movement which helped to bring an end to slavery in the United States began as a religious movement. The civil rights movement had a major element of Christianity involved. I will not apologize for using my belief in Jesus Christ to further the causes of freedom and equality for all people.

We can not and will not move forward as a nation as long as we are a nation divided, fractured into different parts for the benefit of power hungry megalomaniacs. We are one nation, and that nation is made up of many different parts. I honestly don't want to live in a country made up on only one type of people. While Hitler might have been fine with it, I'm not. It is time to "let freedom ring".

NEW BEGINNINGS

Unlike politicians who are willing to complain about a problem and then never propose any real solutions, I believe that there are solutions available, but the politicians don't want to discuss the solutions because they fear for their jobs. Thus, it seems fitting to begin discussing some solutions.

For any solution to be of effect we need a new Constitution. We need a Constitution where equality among all people is at the core of the document, not an idea tacked on in an amendment. For the United States to come together as one nation in the vision of Dr. King we have to finally put racism to bed, and I see no other way to do that then creating a new Constitution with true democratic ideas at its heart. This prospect of recreating our nation for the benefit of all citizens is one which requires the entire nation, not just select groups. We must create a Constitution representative of everyone. We are one nation made up of hundreds of millions of individuals, of all races, religions, and creeds, and the foundational document creating the government which manages such a nation must at its heart convey this ideal. This new Constitution must be a document future generations can look to for guidance when they are faced with trouble. When future generations are in trouble the last thing they need is to search for guidance in an ambiguous document that provides more questions than answers.

This is not to say the framers of the present Constitution did a bad job, in fact quite the contrary. When this nation was in its infancy, our founding fathers could never have imagined the kinds of issues later generations would face. And the truth is we are faced with the same problem today, we have no means by which to envision what the future holds for our nation. However, this does not relieve us from the responsibility we have to the future. Our forefathers did provide for some changes to be made after the Constitution was written, thus the apparent absence of any language involving slavery. By excluding slavery from the Constitution, with the exception of banning the importation of slaves from Africa after 1808, the door was left open to deal with the issue later. This ambiguity is unfortunately what led to the Civil War.

We have the benefit of hindsight. The framers knew nothing about what a government run by the people should look like. Thomas Jefferson even said as much in a letter to Major John Cartwright in June 1824:

> Our revolution commenced on more favorable ground. It presented us an album on which we were free to write what we pleased. We had no occasion to search into musty records, to hunt up royal

parchments, or to investigate the laws and institutions of a semi-barbarous ancestry.

They had ideas based on a number of European philosophers which helped to guide them as they carved out a new nation. In another letter written to Mr. Samuel Kercheval in July of 1816, Jefferson admits some of the short comings of the founding fathers "[w]e had yet to penetrate to the mother principle, that "governments are republican only in proportion as they embody the will of their people and execute it."" In hindsight we see, just as our founding fathers did, the concept of democracy must be extended to all citizens, not just those who own land or have a certain skin color or gender. We now realize democracy provides for economic opportunities no other form of government has, but with those opportunities come pitfall which must be avoided. Our forefathers did well when they wrote the Constitution we have now, but with the benefit of hindsight I know we can do better.

Now I realize there are some people out there who will inevitably say the Constitution we have works well and was written by our forefathers, it has history behind it, so why should we change it? I would reply by saying our forefathers also rode around in horse drawn buggies and crossed oceans in wind powered ships, should we have continued with those instead of progressing with the times? What element of our society has remained unchanged for close to two and a half centuries other than our government? It appears our nation has moved forward but the government which is designed to provide stability for this same nation has been left lagging behind. We are for all intents and purposes a 21st Century nation being governed according to a 18th Century document.

Earlier in Chapter Five I commented on the idea of the Constitution as the original contract with America. However, this is one contract that has a major flaw. Nowhere in the Constitution is there any provision for performance measures. How are we to decide if the government is doing a good job if we have nothing to measure the government's performance against? The only things which come close to providing performance measurements are public opinion polls which are not provided for in the Constitution. There is a fundamental problem with public opinion polls in that the only thing being measured is the degree to which the citizens approve or disapprove of the actions of the government. Unfortunately, as citizens we are provided our information from news media which can be unreliable and from politicians who are out to protect their own image.

Based on the knowledge at hand it is nearly impossible for the public to make a determination of how well the government is performing. Granted there are other tools out there that can be used to judge the effectiveness of government. We can look at economic indexes, at employment figures, and a host of other statistical information. But does this really provide us with an accurate picture of the state of our government? Or is it more likely that what we see are the results of outside influences having little to do with how the government functions?

We need to spread out the power held by the federal government. I propose a new level of government between the states and the federal level. I envision this as a multi-state regional government. The multi-state regional government would exist as a council-manager form of government made up of elected members from the states within the region. Regions would be made up of 3 to 7 states depending on geographic features, with exceptions for Alaska and Hawaii. For example, the states of Florida, Georgia, Alabama, Mississippi, and Louisiana would make up a region. Due to the fact that these states all share similar issues along the gulf coast, it makes sense to group them together to help deal with issues extending beyond state borders. This way of reorganizing the government has the possibility to allow for quicker action in the case of an emergency. Take for instance the disaster which occurred with Hurricane Katrina. If the multi-regional form of government had been in place there would have been a regional FEMA coordinator working with the regional manager to help coordinate evacuations at the local level and communication between the states and the federal government. This is much better than having a FEMA director in Washington D.C. who is out of touch with the situation at the state and local levels.

This form of government would also allow us to change the way that the federal budget is handled. Instead of having Congress decide the entire budget, the process would be more streamlined. Each individual region would be responsible for sending to Congress the budget requirements for their region. Then Congress would be left to determine how much money could be provided to each region. This is not to say each region would actually get the full amount requested. It might be that a region requests $150 million for highway infrastructure improvements, but all Congress has to give is $80 million. Thus it would be up to the regional council to determine which projects are most needed in terms of public safety, economic development, and so forth. If that is not enough money then let the individual states find ways of raising revenue to pay for some of these issues. This idea is very much in keeping with how our founding fathers saw the Constitution being used. I believe it's much better to have issues involving taxes occur at the local or state level were it is easier for the public to get involved. The current budget process at the federal level leaves little room for public involvement, which is completely unacceptable.

One major advantage of budgeting under this form of government is that members of Congress would be unable to add pork barrel projects into the budget. Instead, all members of Congress would be responsible for is a yes or no vote, and nothing more. It is very possible this form of government would allow for the federal budget to be balanced and for the United States to actually begin paying off some debts. It also limits the ability of corporate lobbyists from having influence on policy makers in the budgeting process.

By limiting congressional involvement in the budgeting process, Congress can begin to focus more on the tasks which are designated to them in the Constitution. The legislative branch should be focused on dealing more with international trade and diplomacy more than with internal issues. It's become clear that the federal government does not have a very firm grasp of the events transpiring outside our nations borders. It didn't take a genius to figure out we were going to be attacked by terrorists. There were members of our armed forces who had been complaining about the need for better counter-terrorism activities for close to two decades before the morning of Sept. 11th 2001. We as a nation need to learn to deal with issues when they arise. This is one case where the teachings of Nicolio Machiavelli would serve us very well[1]. Machiavelli teaches that issues of foreign relations need to be treated like a disease. Think of an international problem as if it were cancer. We all know cancer is easiest to cure when the tumor is still small. However, if you let the tumor grow then before long it can become virtually impossible to cure. Many of the current problems that we face around the world are very similar to this.

We knew in the 1970's that oil supplies had the potential to create a problem, yet we did little to resolve the issue. We knew in the late 70's and early 80's that terrorism was going to be a major problem, yet we did very little to combat it. We knew in the mid 80's that the environment was beginning to suffer, and we did next to nothing. We saw in the late 80s and early 90s that Saddam Hussein was going to be a problem, and we dealt with the problem by imposing sanctions we knew from past experience rarely worked to solve diplomatic issues. Ladies and gentleman, we are in our present situation largely because we have a federal government which has a propensity to procrastinate about matters until the situation is so exacerbated as to need reactions which often time do more harm then good. It is imperative that we remove some of the burden of government from the shoulders of the legislative and executive branches, thus allowing them to deal with some important issues which can't be dealt with by anyone else.

The role of the federal government must be better defined. The Tenth Amendment is pretty clear about the fact that any

---

[1] Before anyone gets any stupid ideas, I am by no means saying our government should be run based on Machiavelli's concepts. I am simply stating in this one isolated case; Machiavelli makes a good point about how nations should deal with foreign affairs.

power not specifically granted to the federal government in the Constitution is automatically delegated to the states. This being the case, will someone please explain to me why we have a Department of Education, a Bureau of Alcohol, Tobacco and Firearms, or Department of Agriculture? Maybe I'm missing something but in reviewing the Constitution I can't seem to find where our founding fathers provided for the federal government to have control over any of these areas. The sad part is those three examples are simply the tip of a massive iceberg of what are borderline unconstitutional powers the federal government has kindly granted itself.

Now, I'm not going to get into exactly how it came to be that the powers laid out in the Constitution were usurped by Congress for various purposes. It didn't occur overnight, but rather is the result of a number of actions by a lot of different people, most of whom were well intentioned. Some of it comes from post-Civil War reconstruction. Some of it was the result of FDR's New Deal policies. Some of it comes from policy entrepreneurship by members of Congress in the years following World War II. There is even some of it resulting from lobbyists who fail to understand the exact nature of the powers Congress has. As I stated I'm not going to get into a long discussion about how this came to be. I'm sure after this book has been published, a professor at some university will write a book discussing the exact history of how the Tenth Amendment got abolished without the citizens becoming aware of it.

Our founding fathers created the Tenth Amendment for a reason, and we're learning the reason the hard way. The intention was to limit the powers the federal government has to exactly those provided in the Constitution, so the federal government could never grow so powerful as to force its will on the states. Unfortunately this is exactly what has occurred. We need look no further than the unfunded mandates which are strangling our state and local governments for proof. Further evidence can be seen in the requirements that must be met in order to receive money from federal grants.

How long do we continue to allow the federal government to abuse the system they have broken? How long do we allow individuals other than the citizens of the United States of America to determine the fate of our country? The ideas laid out in these pages represent but a mere fraction of the serious issue our nation faces. These issues are not down the road, these issues are right here, right now. We are at a major junction in the course of this great experiment in democracy, and I ask my fellow U.S. citizens where do we go from here? Are we willing to take control of our destiny and make the changes necessary to ensure the continuation of democracy for the generations to come? I hope the answer is an emphatic YES!

THE RICH KEEP GETTING RICHER...

Big business is not your friend. I know they put ads out there to make it look like they are working for you and trying to make the world a better place, but the facts of the issue are very different. Big business is out for one thing: to make a profit by any means necessary. If people are injured, or even die, businesses don't care. The bigger a business is the more lawyers and public relations specialist they have to make sure the ramifications of any incidents are minimized as much as possible. Then to make up for what ever losses the company has incurred as a result of mismanagement and other activities that put the public at risk, the company will raise prices on the consumer to make up the difference. We see this practice take place everyday.

It's not bad enough that they cost people money. Some of these companies are making products they know will kill people. Some times it's not just one product; in some cases a single holding corporation has ownership of companies that make multiple products that can have negative results, like tobacco products and alcohol. See, this is what they refer to as "diversification" in the business world, and there can be little doubt that they are diversifying, if they can't kill you with a cigarette then they'll kill you with a drunk driver! However, despite these companies trying to kill citizens, most of you are still buying their products, because in some cases the holding company also has ownership of a major food manufacturer. Here we have an example of a company selling a dangerous product, and then when caught red handed they pushed the responsibility onto the consumer of another product they own.

This is simply one representation of numerous companies in all different industries who engage in this kind of activity. A few years back analysts said there would be a 10% increase in the price of toys as a result of lead paint being found on toys made in China. Insurance companies are notorious for raising rates after a major natural disaster. Seriously, do you think with the billions of dollars the insurance companies have paid out for natural disasters in the last year that your rates won't increase? Utility companies often raise rates if the expected use of their commodity is below normal so that they can make up the profits they lost. Why is it the consumer ends up being the one to pay for companies making bad business decisions? I don't remember a U.S. citizen asking companies to use lead based paints on their toys? The culprits here are more big corporations. It was retailers who told companies to manufacture their toys in China so that the toys cost less and thus the retailers could sell more of them and make more money. Now the retailers will try to place the blame on the consumer, but I really don't buy that. Anyone who ever worked in retail, myself included, can tell you some of the merchandise has a huge mark up, and if the retail outlets wanted to sell it for less all they have to do is be willing to accept a smaller profit. But since that's not acceptable, retailers will continue to demand cheap foreign import products they can sell at a larger profit.

The problem is the government is not able to regulate these industries effectively. This is one of the pitfalls of privatization. By allowing various elements of government to be privatized, the government has gone to bed with big business and now has difficulty regulating those same businesses. Once a business gets its foot in the door of government it becomes difficult to fix the problem. A privatized function results in employees being hired within the business and within the government, thus to end the privatization means people losing jobs. Furthermore, if a company is not getting contracts from the government, then the same company is going to be more reluctant to provide campaign contributions to officials seeking re-election. Add to all of this the fact that once the function was privatized the government often rids itself of anything necessary to performing the function. As a result if the government wants to end privatization then the government must go about reacquiring all of the personnel and material assets required for the function. For example, let's say that a city decides to end privatization of waste removal. Now the city needs to buy new garbage trucks, hire sanitation workers, and find a place to dispose of the household waste. It's obvious that once the government starts down the path of privatization it can be incredibly difficult to return the function to the government.

This is not to say privatization is a bad thing. In fact there are a number of cases where privatization can be extremely useful. Many public services such as sanitation and utilities are excellent candidates for privatization. The initial upfront cost to establish these types of services can be cost prohibitive for many cities. As a result, the government can contract out the service to a private firm who already has the resources. In the long run privatization of this type saves the citizens money; with the only major pitfall being the potential for a lack of accountability on the part of the company. However the lack of accountability is a major pitfall because once the company is well establish in performing the function they have the government over a barrel and by extension the citizens. Often times these contracts can be big enough to make or break a business. As a result, the company knows they have a monopoly on their particular service, thus they don't have to worry as much about accountability to the government. It is interesting to note that Jefferson wanted language in the Constitution limiting monopolies. If the trash company isn't doing a good job, what is the city to do? If there's another trash company, then you can change companies, but otherwise the only options are to continue with the status quo or have the city take over the function which can cost a large sum of money.

As stated, there are some cases where privatization is good, but there is always a risk involved. There are also cases where privatization should never be considered an option. Privatization is never a good option when the safety of the public is of concern. The risk to the public is inversely proportional to the benefits of privatization. The higher the risk to the public the lower the potential benefits of privatizing a government function. Thus it only makes sense that functions related to national defense, public safety and transportation should not be privatized. Just ask yourself, do you want private security providing for law enforcement in your community? The obvious answer is no; it is much better to have a professional police department to provide for public safety as opposed to a private security firm with limited accountability. However, in a strange twist, this is exactly what happened in Iraq with companies like KBR Halliburton and Blackwater. Even now some of the activities these private security firms were engaged in while working in Iraq are being investigated. I guess that someone missed the comment Machiavelli made about mercenaries, and how they only work for money and have no loyalty to the government.

I feel the need to reiterate that there is a place in government for private businesses. Earlier I discussed a plan that would allow for new social security cards that would double as debit cards in times of emergency. Since the government is not set up to provide these types of services, it only makes sense for the U.S. government to contract with one of the major credit card companies to create and distribute these cards. The activation of the cards and the administration of the program would be controlled by the Department of Homeland Security, but the cards could be manufactured by a credit card company. The emergency supplies I discussed would have to be transported by motor carrier or railroad. Clearly there is a place in government for the private sector, but we need to be very careful about the role the private sector takes.

A lot of the problems existing within our government are the result of capitalism. This is not to say capitalism is all together bad because it's not. However capitalism left completely unchecked is always fatal to democracies. Democracy depends on, in Alexander Hamilton's words "the consent of the people". With capitalism an interesting transformation begins to take place. Our nation started out as a representative democracy. As time has gone by some individuals began to amass wealth and with wealth came power. Now, the power the elite have attained through wealth had to have come from some where, there is no power fairy who sprinkles pixie dust on people and they magically get powers from no where. The elite actually get their power from the people by using their wealth to lobby politicians who are supposed to be representing the best interest of all the citizens. The elite use their wealth to buy high power attorneys to make sure they have limited exposure to liability when things go wrong. In essence they use wealth to ensure their security with no thought for the rest of society.

This problem isn't new, in fact its actually part of the evolutionary process of government. Governments exist on a sort of continuum which stretches from dictators and tyrants to representative monarchies to representative democracies and finally to plutocracies. The result is a continuum bracketed by two different versions of absolute power, one being the result of fear and the other the result of wealth. In looking at history we can see this progression. The British Empire began under an absolute monarch where the king derived power from the divine right to rule. After the signing of the Magna Carta we see the transition to a more representative monarchy. With the American Revolution we see the development of a representative democracy in the North American colonies. And finally today we see the development of a plutocracy run by the wealth elites of society. As wealth increases so does power, but to want extent remains unclear in that there has to be a limit to the amount of power the people are willing to give up to the wealthy. We have long seen the government as "Big

Brother" but in reality Corporate America is taking on that role at an alarming rate.

The question becomes when will the people decide they have given up enough power and decide to take it back, and in what form will this occur? History shows us that often times these kinds of situations often end up badly. Unfortunately, most nations trying to reign in the powerful elite end up in a protracted civil war and eventually are back at the other end of the continuum being ruled by a dictator of some sort. A good example of this would be seen in the French Revolution. The key difference being that France was a monarchy at the time of the revolution, but the aftermath was the same none the less. For all the good intentions politicians seem to have regarding the "Arab Spring" movement, history shows us that it's much more likely that these nations will end up with a government worse than the one they overthrew.

Corporate America in many ways dictates how we live our lives. Some time back I read a job posting on the internet where a company stated "let's face it, we live in a brand loyalty world". Clearly somewhere along the way corporations in this country got things wrong. Let me explain how a company is ideally to go about creating brand loyalty. A company that provides good services, high quality products, at a reasonable price generates business, and as the company continues to do so their consumer base grows. Now let's look at how companies actually go about creating brand loyalty today. A company provides really bad services; a horrible product that might end up being recalled as defective, charges an exorbitant price and then hires a marketing firm to use psychology to trick consumers into buying something they don't need. Do you really need the latest, greatest techno-gadget or did you just get conned by the marketing idiots?

Let there be no doubt marketing professionals, I hesitate to use the term "professional" for borderline criminal activity, are well versed in getting you to buy what you don't need. Strategically place a product in a romantic movie and lonely people will buy the product hoping the product will end their loneliness. It worked for the character in the movie, why won't it work for them? These people think like criminals. They prey on the public just like some perverted sexual predator. People in marketing make me sick because they look to prey on the weakest members in society. They prey on people who suffer from depression, who are lonely, feel inadequate, they prey on children. Seriously, what kind of scum preys on a child to make money?

I want to take a moment to discuss good businesses. The fact is, we have some very good businesses in the United States. Unfortunately, we see too often the negative surface. The nature of our media does not provide for coverage of businesses who do the right thing. Far too often we hear CEOs trying to justify something they did which had a negative impact on society. Even today we have CEOs who continue to argue that the economic troubles our nation is faced with are the fault of the U. S. consumer as opposed to the failures of big business. Nothing could be further from the truth. With that said there are responsible companies out there.

I am a die hard fan of Oakley. Not only does Oakley provide a superior product to that offered by their competitors, but the management at Oakley is willing to take a stand for what's right. A perfect example of this comes from Lance Armstrong who after being diagnosed with cancer was kicked off his cycling team. Left without medical insurance it was Oakley's CEO who stepped up and provided Armstrong with insurance coverage through his company. Oakley continues to employ U.S. citizens. I own a number of pairs of Oakley's and each pair says "Made in the U.S.A.". We can only hope the same good will extends to the rest of the corporation to which Oakley now belongs.

Along with my Oakley's whenever I go outdoors I tend to take an Osprey backpack of some sort with me. Most people have never heard of Osprey, a small outdoors equipment company located in Cortez, Colorado. Osprey makes it a point to give back to the community, even going so far as to provide employees extra paid vacation days to help clean up the environment and volunteer in their community. Osprey is another one of those companies who proudly proclaims to be "Made in the U.S.A.".

Blackhawk is in my opinion the absolute best tactical equipment provider for military and law enforcement. Blackhawk is a company founded by warriors and dedicated to providing those who put their lives on the line the best equipment that can be had. Blackhawk has repeatedly stepped in and filled a void in the equipment needs of U.S. troops around the world. While it might be true that we have to fight wars with the equipment at hand, Blackhawk makes sure the equipment our troops have available is the best possible.

The list goes one, but we unfortunately don't hear the success stories of these companies as often as we hear of the failures of other companies. It's time for our money to follow our ethics when choosing a company to do business with. If we continue to do business with companies who are not willing to be partners with the citizens then we will see further economic failures. The current failures in our economy are not the result of the short comings of the U.S. consumer, but rather the result of the parasitic nature of big business.

Earlier I discussed how capitalism was ultimately fatal to a republican form of government. Our current economic crisis highlights the cause for this fatal nature. Capitalism is never allowed to truly function as the sole economic platform within a democracy. Under capitalism if a business is under performing the business ultimately fails, and another comes along to take its place. Instead of true capitalism we get a hybrid of capitalism and socialism. The Obama administration's plan for reorganizing General Motors and Chrysler called for the redistribution of the companies to various stakeholders, with the labor union get a disproportionately large share. Once we begin redistribution of wealth we are dealing with socialist and communist ideals.

This is not to say Corporate America is not to blame for some of this. I'll again pull from the headlines to illustrate the point. A few years ago I read an article discussing how auto insurance companies are planning to raise insurance rates because of Chrysler and General Motors bankruptcy, claiming the parts for these makes and models will be more difficult to get for repairs. The problem is, this is all a lie. We all know that bankruptcy does not mean the company completely ceases to exist. Both of these companies will continue to make parts for some years to come and there is no reason for the insurance companies to be raising rates except to increase their profit margin. I wonder how long until we see a rise in medical insurance rates due to some new disease?

The banking industry is just as bad about this as the insurance industry. We have banks getting hand outs from the U.S. government at incredible low interest rates and the banks are responding by rating interest rates on credit cards or canceling people's second mortgage altogether. The price of a barrel of oil can go down and yet the price of a gallon of gasoline will go up. This isn't about inflation or a troubled economy. It's about one word: greed. Greed is an evil disease that has infected the large part of this country, and I will talk about greed later and how it involves our government.

It's funny how companies seem to always find a way to blame consumers for their poor business performance. In reality it's the fault of business "leaders" who don't know what they're doing. We see this on the news everyday; we see groups claiming the actions of consumers are the cause of all their woes when in reality it's the practices of the business or even the industry as a whole are causing the problem. Generally speaking I have gone to great lengths to not name specific companies as I don't feel it serves any purpose to call a company out on the carpet over issues they already know exist. However, this is one case where I will make an exception. The entertainment industry is without a doubt the best example of an industry blaming the consumers for their own management short comings. Specifically the RIAA and the MPAA have been rather blatant in their abuse of the consumers. These two groups have used peer-to-peer file sharing as a scapegoat to draw attention away from the fact that they are not providing quality merchandise. Now I'm one of the people who actually buy CDs and DVDs. In the last 12 months I've purchased 10 CDs, and all but two of those CDs were by dead artists. Is it the consumer's fault a CD with ten songs only has two songs that are worth listening to?

Better yet, since the RIAA and the MPAA wanted to bring up the issue of theft and copyright laws; let's talk about how they break those laws on a regular basis. These two groups are notorious for releasing "collector's editions", "limited editions", and other boxed sets containing the same material as a previous release but with some bonus material to entice the consumer. Someone tell me why I have to pay for material I already own the "fair use rights" to in order to get the new material?

That's not the only way that the entertainment industry has found to make money on the same merchandise twice. The reality is that Corporate America is trying to redefine what it means to have ownership. Groups like the RIAA are looking for every way possible to make more money at the expense of the consumer. As the RIAA sees it, you only own the CD, not the "fair use rights" to the music on the CD. Now we see the real reason the RIAA went after peer-to-peer file sharing so viciously. RIAA member companies didn't want MP3 to succeed. For decades they have made billions of dollars off the sale of greatest hit's and box set CDs featuring little in the way of new material. Now the defense the RIAA and others in the entertainment industry will undoubtedly use is that no one forces you to buy the music. While it's true no one is putting a gun to the consumers head, at the same time the marketing practices they are employing tend to say other wise.

The question we really need to be asking is where does this redefining of ownership lead us in the future? Are we going to get to the point where banks tell people they no longer own their home, only the right to live there? Furthermore, you won't be allowed to remodel the home, but you'll have to buy a new one. Will we get to the point where people no longer own their car, but only the right to drive it, and instead of repairing your car when it breaks down you'll have to buy a new one? This would represent a major boom for all industries, if you no longer own it there are no concerns for warranties. This means companies can make defective products and not have to worry about repairing them and possibly have an out when it comes to the resulting lawsuits. I would hope after reading this every one of the attorneys who went after big tobacco will begin filing civil suits against the RIAA and the MPAA on behalf of the U.S. consumers.

I want to take a moment to get at the real cause of our nations failing economy. Let's take a moment to look at a little business practice known as networking. Networking is when you use your friends and family members to help you get a job. In reality networking is the politically correct term for nepotism, and nepotism is the nice way of saying corporate incest. See this is one of the reasons so many companies in the U.S. are in trouble. Instead of hiring people who have fresh ideas, these companies hire the friends and family members of their employees. Networking also means businesses are hiring new employees who have already heard all of the horror stories and will be predisposed to bad performance. Thus Corporate America is not hiring the best and the brightest, but some of the dumbest people available. If you work in human resources and use "networking" as a hiring tool, you are sabotaging your company, and if you're a CEO whose HR department is using this tool you need to start firing some people.

Another interesting hiring practice is to hire based on experience more than education. Let me see if I can explain this as simply as possible. If you are hiring people with past experience, then you are hiring the past for your company.

Industries move forward, industries evolve, but if you're only hiring people who have past experience then the company is held hostage to the past. By hiring people base on past performance companies always have an easy out. Instead of fixing the problem by hiring the most qualified candidate who will help to ensure the future of the company, the powers that be will claim the consumer is the problem and then pay some marketing firm to create a new gimmick. Then there is the fail safe plan that involves the Board of Directors forcing a CEO out while paying the same CEO a bundle of money as part of a severance package. Multi-million dollar severance packages are a prime example of what is wrong with Corporate America. No one in their right mind would pay someone millions of dollars as a reward for running a successful company into the ground! It sounds to me more like these companies are paying the trouble maker to go away. Let's call it like it is, its not a severance package, its more like legalized extortion.

Furthermore, why do executive get high dollar retirement funds? Is it just me or doesn't it seem reasonable for these same executives to be in charge of saving for their own retirement? Seriously, if these executives don't have enough skills with money to save for their own retirement; then what are they doing running multi-million dollar corporations? CEOs of publicly traded companies should be held to the same standard as politicians when it comes to ethics. Unfortunately, the powerful lobbyists corporations hired by Corporate America would see to it that those kinds of progressive laws are never considered.

While it might not seem like it, there is a good reason for why Corporate America doesn't function like the rest of the nation.

CORPORATE AMERICA:
IT'S LIKE A WHOLE OTHER COUNTRY

Today there is a corporate culture of corruption that is pervasive throughout the United States. Corporate America is determined to remake the United States of America in its own twisted image. Many authors have written recently about the war that is being waged against the middle class in the United States. There is some truth to this fact, the upper class is trying to drive a deeper divide between themselves and the middle class. However, the far more ominous issue is how Corporate America is waging war on individuality and the identity of the United States citizen. The ultimate goal is a nation populated by mindless automatons who willingly buy what ever corporations are selling. The assault on individuality is a war in every sense of the term. We are under attack from every side. Corporate America is not content with destroying individuality today, but the concept of individuality in the past and the future.

To some degree it makes sense for companies to seek to curtail individuality. The more individuality there is, the greater the variety of products that has to be produced. The dream of every CEO is a "one size fits all" society where companies can mass produce products at a fraction of the cost and sell them in local discount retailers. This is the retail discount model: make as few a varieties as cheap as possible and sell them at a discounted cost. Most companies don't like the idea of consumers having a wide range of choices. This is the goal of marketing, to create a "buzz" around a product so everyone wants it, because if you don't have the new "it" product you won't fit in with society.

The business community is attacking our individuality in ways that we don't even consider. Part of the sense of self every person has is based on history, both personal and cultural. For example, the Bureau of Land Management is tasked with protecting public lands so the environmental and cultural nature of the land is preserved. Unfortunately the BLM has decided it is more advantageous to allow big business to exploit this land for profit by drilling for oil and natural gas. There are currently tens of thousands of sites of archaeological significance in the southwest United States which are being destroyed for the profit of big business. I truly hope destroying the cultural heritage of the Native American people is worth all the money they are making.

This is a good example of how business is destroying individuality. It' not uncommon for people to tie who they are to their cultural identity based on the past. More than just attacking individuality, we are allowing businesses to destroy the cultural heritage of our nation. How are we going to teach our children about the past so they better understand where we have come from if we destroy any remnant the past ever existed? These sites are important and a clear message needs to be sent to the business community that destroying our nation's cultural heritage will not be tolerated.

The problem of destroying history is further compounded by business doing more than destroying the physical reminders of our history; some businesses actually attempt to rewrite history. There have been many books written about the lies and other factual inaccuracies being taught to school children today, and it doesn't serve my purpose to cover ground many have already touched upon. None the less we need to make sure the past accomplishments and failures of the United States are preserved in such a way that future generations can learn from them. If a company was responsible for using slave labor prior to the Civil War then admit to doing so. Now this is not to say the companies should be subject to frivolous lawsuits meant to make the descendants of slaves rich. If you wish to file suit against a company for using slavery, then you need to provide documentary evidence the company enslaved the actual living plaintiff in violation of the 13th Amendment. Someone's great-great-great grandfather being enslaved during the early 1800's in what was a very disgusting social institution is not reason for someone today to get rich.

Businesses don't limit their destruction of individuality to history, they extend it to families. In many cases the business model is not designed for the family. This is another area where the entertainment industry has sought to devalue our society. Television doesn't provide a good example of a family. We have music the makes the life of a dead beat dad seem glorious. Now I realize that there are a lot of people who are going to take issue with this and claim there are all kinds of families out there and people shouldn't be required to fit into a societal ideal of a family. Generally speaking I agree there shouldn't be any expectation of a societal ideal for a family. There is a problem with this concept however. What is considered to be the societal ideal is being influenced by the media. According to the U.S. Department of Health and Human Services the number of single parent households rose to 28% in 2002 from 20% in 1980. This period coincides with the period when the entertainment industry began to push the idea on the public.

Our young people are watching and listening to media that promotes a man as being a "player". Some members of the business community market this idea with slogans like "don't hate the player, hate the game". Since these companies don't seem to understand the damage they are doing to society let me provide them with a little glimpse. In 2002 statistics show that 44% of all African American children were being raised in single mother households. That means the mother was acting as the main influence in her child's life. The mother is working to put food on the table, to provide for what her children need. How does this mother have time to be an individual? How does this mother have time to be an active member of society? Furthermore the rest of society must help pick up the pieces by providing medical care and funding for schools and other essentials. The single mother is doing all she can while some idiot little boy, I refuse to dignify them by referring to them as men, runs around being a "player". But what else are they supposed to be, they've been told it's the best lifestyle to live.

The leaders of the business community are also looking to destroy our government. One of the most disturbing trends in government today is the revolving door that is the Office of

Personnel Management. The scam seems to work like this, the upper level of management in the federal government works for a few years and then transitions to the private sector where they take advantage of all the problems they created in the agency they just left. Then after a few years in the private sector they return to the federal government to create some more problems only to return to the public sector thus starting the cycle all over again. Only the business community could conceive of a plan like this. I'll give them this it's absolutely ingenious. I can think of no better way to create a condition where the person who created a problem can then be paid massive amounts of money as a contractor to correct the same problem.

I've talked at length about the damage business is doing. The corrupt nature of Corporate America is in reality the result of a cause and effect relationship. The leadership of Corporate America is based on the training individuals receive while working on a Master's of Business Administration, or MBA. I believe every problem facing the world today can in some way, shape or form be traced back to someone with an MBA. This training seems to be centered on training people to attack individuality, putting the profit margin of the company before anything else, and attacking democracy at every opportunity. I'm starting to think MBA actually stands for Master of Beelzebub's Arts.

The key item drilled into the heads of people in MBA programs is the need for a competitive advantage. Unfortunately, this competitive advantage doesn't end with the business community, but extends to all aspects of society. They look for ways to maintain the competitive advantage over the government and by extension over the citizens. The

112

problem is the competitive advantage corporations are looking for means the degradation of the people's ability to govern society. The social norms of a society help to dictate the direction the society will progress. However, as a result of competitive advantage, Corporate America is dictating the direction society moves.

Social norms help to drive society by creating ideas of what individuals are expected to do within the confines of society. Corporate America changes this by driving society through different agents than social norms. These agents of change are no longer human interaction, but financial and business concerns. For example, social norms hold that polluting is not a responsible activity for an individual, as can be seen in various littering and emissions control laws. Social norms, as an agent of change helped to pass laws protecting the environment. Big business is not concerned with protecting the environment, but with how much profit can be made. Since proper environmental stewardship would cut into the profit margin, it's not acceptable for companies to enact environmentally friendly policies unless it will make them money.

Many authors have written entire books about the idea of norms of reciprocity and the impact on society. To put it in simple terms, norms of reciprocity constitutes the interactions that take place between individuals. In other words a norm of reciprocity is a complicated way of saying the Golden Rule. If you do good to others they will reciprocate in kind. Society generally operates under this set of rules to great effect. Unfortunately, Corporate America doesn't function under these rules. Norms of reciprocity hold that if you don't try to kill another person, they probably won't try to kill you, and if they do they will face consequences. Corporate America believes they should be able to manufacture a product they know will kill a person, and then market the product to people. This is the case with tobacco products. While social norms dictate you don't manufacture the product, business norms dictate you manufacture it, but make as much money as you can before the people can die from it. That's what nicotine is all about, making the product as addictive as possible so the tobacco industry can make as much money as possible before the victim, I mean consumer, dies.

This might seem like a minor issue, but in reality it represents a major problem. The reason big business attacks individuality is big business doesn't understand individuality. Companies don't market to individuals, but to demographics. In the mass production world of Corporate America there is simply no room for the existence of the individual. Individuality costs more money versus a highly standardized society. Think in terms of retail sales. Say I was to go shopping for a new dress shirt. I have three choices. First, I could go to a local discount retailer (Wal-Mart, K-Mart, Target, which ever you prefer) and I would most likely find shirts in a few different colors and styles, priced very reasonably and available in sizes small, medium, large and extra large. My second choice would be to go to a department store (Macy's, Dillard's, Nordstrom's and so forth) where I would find dress shirts costing more, but are available in a much wider variety of styles, colors and sizes. My third choice would be to go to a tailor and have a dress shirt made to fit me in the color and style of fabric I desire, but at a higher cost. As you can see, the more individualized the choice, the more it costs. Companies are willing to sacrifice individuality for a profit. After all, it's not their individuality they are sacrificing; CEOs have the money to buy individuality.

Society on the other hand seems to have a tendency to embrace individuality. That's what social norms help to establish. Social norms are the agent by which people become self aware and thus individuals. Society is comprised of a sort of equilibrium, where individuals seek to express their individuality while at the same time blend in with the accepted social norms. The different ways people seek to accomplish this task is part of what makes someone a unique individual. Most of the major elements of society have an individual aspect to them. Most religions embrace a certain amount of individuality. In Christianity, for example, we see the idea of individuality embraced in 1 Corinthians 12, where Paul discusses the different parts of the church and how they work together as one. Truth be known, if everyone were the same, society wouldn't function.

Businesses are the exact opposite in many ways. The last thing a business wants is an individual. As the saying goes, "there is no "I" in team". Beginning with the industrial revolution, business started to function like a machine, where every part is designed to perform a designated function and no part is designed to function independently of the other parts. The perfect society or business would be one that consisted of an organizational structure where individual traits are embraced for the greater good. This becomes almost a form or Utilitarianism, where you seek the greatest possible benefit for the greatest number of people. Funny thing, that sounds a lot like how government is designed to work. Actually if you think about it, this makes a certain amount of sense. Business learned to function like a machine as a result of the industrial revolution. Society functions much more on the individual level, with each person acting independent of others, yet still dependent on others for social interaction. Government becomes a combination of these two ideas, the utilitarian bureaucracy which tries to do the most good for the greatest number of citizens while working in highly compartmentalized agencies that have difficulty dealing with individual variations within the services which need to be provided.

One of the most disturbing aspects of the interaction between the government and Corporate America is the degree to which corporations are willing to abuse the government, and by extension the citizens, to meet their own goals. Let's look at an example of how corporations abuse the government. A very popular form of financing designed to spur local development is what's referred to as tax increment financing (TIF). The basic idea behind TIF is simple, as land is developed (or redeveloped) the property value of the surrounding area increases, thus increasing the amount of revenue available though property taxes. The increased tax revenue is then used to pay the debt incurred during the development of the land. TIF was designed to provide for economic incentives for development of land that would otherwise go undeveloped or redevelopment of blighted areas. Generally speaking tax increment financing has worked well. Through the use of this finance method we've seen the redevelopment of the urban core of many major metropolitan areas.

Unfortunately, in recent years developers and major corporations have begun to abuse TIF to meet their own goals. For example, we see suburban areas that would be developed without a TIF, being granted one to help offset the

116

development cost. Add into this scenario the extension of tax abatements for the same development and you have a city where the citizens are helping to foot the bill for a development they will not see any benefit from for years. The most egregious offender here seems to be retailers, and particularly big box retailers. Big box retailers often seem to do more harm than good for a community. We're talking about companies, who seek the TIF, and the tax abatement, plus they fail to pay their employees a wage above poverty level, and they fail to provide adequate benefits such as medical insurance. What we're left with is a community where the tax payers are helping to pay for the development, seeing a reduced benefit for a while, plus being burdened with providing low income, section 8 housing for the store's employees (and the decrease in property values associated with section 8 housing), and helping to pay for medical care since the employees have no benefits.

The issue with TIF abuse is unfortunately only the tip of the iceberg. For years the telecom industry received tax breaks from the federal government to help offset the cost of providing high speed, broadband data services to the citizens of the United States. We look at DSL and cable modems as if they're fast, but in reality our tax dollars went to pay for T1 and T3 lines we don't have. The telecom industry simply took the money and then never made good on their end of the bargain. Furthermore the telecom industry is far from the sole offender. There are numerous companies who overcharge the government. It's not uncommon for companies to win a bid on a government contract and get half way done with the contract before file a notice with the government that the cost of the service has unexpectedly increased. I've heard of companies filing three or more notices of cost increase. I

117

seriously doubt companies are unable to accurately bid the cost of a project.

Is it just me, or does it seem to anyone else like the tax payers of this nation are being looked upon to bear an unfair burden for Corporate America's success? It seems the real meaning behind the terms "profit margin" and "bottom line" is this: Corporate America wants to make as much money from the consumers, as fast as possible before the product they make kills the same consumer. Let's look at the examples before us: alcohol, tobacco, defective drugs, poisoned toys, tainted pet food, and unsafe cars just to name a few products. This doesn't sound like capitalism, it sounds more like genocide, and truth be known it might not be far from the next step for some companies.

THE COLD HARD TRUTH

I realize that these last two chapters have been a lot. Furthermore, I realize the greedy, money grubbing, pathetic excuses for human beings who inhabit the upper echelons of Corporate America will be attacking the statements I've made in the previous chapters in a vain attempt to salvage what ever miniscule amount of respect they might have left. In fact they will probably begin to complain that I'm using hyperbole and scare tactics to get people to believe the ideas I'm putting forth. So, in an attempt to cut them off at the pass and minimize any damage they can do, I've decided to launch the literary equivalent of a preemptive strike by using a developing issue in the United States to illustrate the points made in the previous chapters.

Some time ago there was an article in the Chicago Tribune and an article by Bob Sullivan on MSNBC.com which helped to shed light on an impending problem involving the use of credit reports in regards to medical care. Fair Isaac, a major credit reporting firm, began a business venture under the corporate name Healthcare Analytics. Since the story was published Fair Isaac renamed the company Connance. The purpose of Connance is to create a means by which hospitals, insurance companies and doctors can access the credit information of their patients. The goal of Connance is to track uninsured and self pay individuals who seek medical care and insure collection of payment through a web based system. The obvious question is: why does the health care industry need to access credit ratings?

Connance claims this is to allow hospitals and doctors offices to make determinations about billing and other business functions. The problem is we can't be sure of how far this will go. Will we see them combining our credit record with our medical history? If so it provides for the nightmare scenario where the health insurance companies could turn a person down for coverage based on a combination of personal and financial reasons. The insurance companies could begin to blacklist individuals to prevent them from getting coverage.

Connance also claims their product would only be used after the patient had received treatment. However, as many opponents are pointing out, there is no regulatory device to ensure patient treatment will be preserved. In an article publishing in July 2009 on Allbusiness.com, Connance's Chief Development Officer David Franklin said the following:

> About 40% of self-pay accounts have too
> thin a credit file to generate a credit bureau score, so
> health care providers can't look at a patient's credit
> bureau score or income as the sole predictor of their
> ability to pay… Scoring models built from health care

> data help predict the expected value of the account once it goes into collections and develop the right treatment to maximize recovery and the cost of the treatment strategy.

In other words, the model will be used to determine the course of care ("right treatment") based on the credit score and the patients expected ability to pay ("maximum recovery"). Connance has no way of ensuring the hospital won't look up the information first and provide someone with substandard care based on their credit rating, or worse, deny them care altogether. Let's face it, the health care industry is a business and they will do what is necessary to ensure they make a profit, and if it means someone dies because of a low credit rating then so be it.

The use of credit ratings to determine care opens a Pandora's Box of potential problems. We end up in the same situation we're in with the use of credit reports as a means of judging employability. Individuals who are sick and have gone into debt to fight the illness or those who have lost their job and have no medical insurance are the people in need the most, but based on credit scores would be the first to go without care. Now Connance counters by claiming federal law prevents anyone from being denied medical care, and they are absolutely right. However, as we have seen before, the power of businesses to hire lobbyists means the law can change at a moments notice. The health care industry could easily hire lobbyist to repeal that federal law and leave citizens at the mercy of Corporate America in time of need.

Unfortunately, all the problems described above aren't the scariest part of using credit scores in medical care. Let's speculate here for a moment and say the worst case scenario happens: the credit scores are used to determine care, the laws requiring care are revoked and citizens are at the mercy of the health care industry. Remember that discussion earlier in Chapter 5 about using credit scores to as a basis for employment and how minorities have a tendency to have lower credit scores because of lower wage jobs and lower levels of post secondary education? Well, now what would happen if credit scores were used to determine medical care? It would mean that minorities, immigrants, people with disabilities and others would receive little or no medical care. We're talking about some citizens of The United States of America being left to suffer and die. The scariest part of the tool that Connance has developed is how easily it can become a tool of genocide. I'm not saying the tool will be used for this purpose, but do we really want a tool out there that can be? Given Corporate American's reckless behavior in recent years shouldn't we expect the worse?

What about the use of the medical records by other companies? What is to ensure an individual's medical record won't be issued to a prospective employer and in turn someone could be turned down for a job because of a history of mental illness or some other health issue? There is no guarantee these kinds of scenarios won't take place, and you can be sure Connance will see to it that there are laws passed to protect them from litigation if a "mistake" were to occur. So not only would at risk populations be at the mercy of companies, but now the general public would have to worry about their own ability to gain employment. It's quite possible people would stop going to doctors out of fear of losing their jobs. Deaths from conditions like cancer could skyrocket because people stopped getting the preventive screening tests done because they don't want to lose their job or not be offered a job in the future based on a medical condition.

What about people who are diagnosed with cancer or some other fatal illness? Does a person's credit rating have an effect on the level of care they receive? Earlier I discussed the idea of individuality costing money, and the more you have to spend the greater the degree of individuality you can attain. It could easily be that people who have better credit ratings will have access to more experimental treatments and other types of therapy while those with less money have no access to those same potentially life saving treatments. All citizens should have the right to access the same level of care for a medical condition regardless of the amount of money they have.

The program Connance is developing is meant to serve no other purpose than to fulfill their desire to make more money. The idea to use credit reports in the health care field is being developed on a foundation of greed at an extreme level. This isn't about helping patients recover from a serious illness. This idea is about developing a product with the sole intention of making a profit without any concern for the harm it may do to citizens as a result. Medical credit reports have the potential to do more harm than good.

I pulled this topic from the headlines to illustrate the very real nature of the problems we as a nation face. I readily admit the descriptions above represent the worst case scenario. However, when dealing with Corporate America, we must expect the worst and hope for the best. From tainted pet food, toys painted with lead based paints, to criminal financial mismanagement of businesses; time and again we have seen these types of problems arise. Corporate America has yet to prove they are responsible enough to be trusted by the public with this type of power, and yet they're trying to take it anyway. The government has yet to prove it has the ability to provide adequate oversight to check the power required for such a tool to be used.

Here we are right back at the idea of checks and balances. The problems inherent with medical credit reports illustrate the larger problems with the system of checks and balances. If the amount of power being granted is so concentrated and the group it's being given to so irresponsible, that we feel the need to provide for a checking mechanism, then we need to reconsider if they should have the power to begin with. Once again, the checks and balances system is not a system of government but a fail safe device. The health care industry is quick to point to the fact that hospitals are burdened by the impoverished and uninsured. However, those same individuals in the health care industry fail to point out the hospitals are a major part of the problem. Hospitals are notorious for over charging for services. A test costing $40 at your doctor's office will cost $400 at a hospital. Most states have consumer protection laws which prohibit "gross overcharging for products and services". Of course, the hospitals have powerful teams of lawyers to ensure they are never held accountable for violating those laws. What good are laws if the laws aren't enforceable? The development of medical credit reports is not about insuring our nation's health, but about insuring the rich people's wealth.

Here we are back at the issue of the government's failure to establish justice. It's injustices perpetrated by the business community that have caused the kinds of problems the health care industry is complaining about. It's the government's inability to provide a fair and equal distribution of justice which has provided the opportunity for unethical and illegal business practices to thrive.

When discussing the topic of domestic tranquility I touched on the issue of the citizens not trusting the government. The fact that the government is looking the other way while Corporate America makes an attempt to potentially deny medical care to those who need it most illustrates why the citizens have lost trust in the government. Medical credit reports are not representative of the will of the U.S. citizen, but the desires of the greedy business executives. If the government elected by the citizens has no ability to properly regulate business to ensure the needs of the citizens are being met, then why should the citizens trust the government?

From the stand point of providing a common defense, what happens if we institute medical credit reports and they are used to determine care, and after all of this has occurred there is a terrorist attack using a chemical or biological weapon? The use of medical credit reports could result in citizens of lower incomes being denied care after the attack. Let's forget about the terrorist for a moment and say there was another influenza epidemic; would the impoverished receive health care then? The health care industry represents an important element of our nation's common defense. The structural elements of our nation's national security apparatus stretch far beyond the military industrial complex. This is a lesson the United States should have learned from the casualties which occurred during the Civil War. If a bloody and protracted war where a lot of people died because of insufficient medical care doesn't prove the connection between defense and medicine, I don't know what does. I fear the day that a global pandemic could result in some of Connance's technology being used exactly as I

125

described. What better example do I need to provide of the very real nature of this threat.

The connection between health care and the general welfare mentioned in the preamble seems obvious. Remember in Chapter 5 the discussion about politicians wanting to mandate health insurance? The product being developed by Connance is the exact tool the health insurance companies would use to determine risk in the case of mandatory insurance requirements. I think it's also interesting that the first state to create the idea of mandatory health insurance was Massachusetts, and Connance is based in Massachusetts. I seriously doubt both Connance being based there and the State of Massachusetts mandating medical insurance represent a simple coincidence. It sound to me more likely that Connance provided lobbyists to push the insurance mandate through the Massachusetts state house to insure Connance had a readily available group of consumers when their product hit the open market.

While we're at it, think of the horrifying way the Connance system could be used by the government for President Obama's socialized health care. It's well know at this point that our government is notorious for over paying for products and services. The same will hold true of a national health care program. Thus being the case, how will the government pay for everyone's health care when they're over paying for so much of it? The fact is some people are going to have to be denied care. So how is the government going to make the determination on who gets denied care? Simple, the government will use the tools already at their disposal, tools like those developed by Connance. President Obama's health care plan needs an FDA black box warning label. They'll take your money, deny you care, and watch you die. Welcome to healthcare related genocide.

The issues revolving around the use of health care credit reports serves to further highlight the issue of big business using lobbyist to advance their agendas in government with complete disregard for what is in the best interest of the citizens. Medical credit reports provide a clear window into the intentions of Corporate America to abuse the greed of politicians to the best of their ability. Since corporations function based on greed, they feel right at home using lobbyists to buy control of the nation. Let there be no doubt buying control is exactly what we are talking about. Business is all about control: controlling the markets, controlling production, controlling consumers, and so on, and the amount of control seems to be tied to the amount of money spent. Corporate America has become accustom to the idea of waving some money under the noses of politicians and getting their way. Unfortunately, this type of lobbying is slowly eroding the fabric of democracy in the United States. It is imperative that lobbying be brought under some type of control, and the government regulates the practice to insure the best interest of the citizens is the primary concern in any government endeavor.

SO WHAT NOW?

As we near the conclusion it seems the problems our nation is facing have become obvious. However, for the sake of clarity let's review:

1. We need a new Constitution which solves some of the problems present with the
current document. The new Constitution needs to return the power of government to the people. As Alexander Hamilton said in the *Federalist Papers* "[t]he fabric of American Empire ought to rest on the solid basis of the CONSENT OF THE
PEOPLE." We cannot return the government to the people as long as corporations, lobbyists and special interest groups are dictating policy.

2. We must create solid performance measures by which we can gauge the quality of the work the government is doing. How can we expect to create

better government if we have no idea of how well the government is doing the job to begin with?

3. We must dissolve the barriers still existing in our society. We are one nation and it's high time we begin to act like it. We are still a house divided, and until we come to terms with ending discrimination we cannot move forwards as a nation.

4. We must take responsibility for our future. It's up to us to make sure the needs of this nation are able to be met in the future. This means we need to ensure quality education for future generations, good stewardship of the environment, protection from foreign aggressors, and the continuation of freedoms in this nation.

5. We must provide for the welfare of all citizens. We are one nation and we have to learn to help each other more. We need to ensure access to health care and security in the event of an emergency. The United States will only be as strong as its weakest link, and these two issues represent serious weaknesses.

If we don't come to terms and deal with these issues we will have problems in the future. We can see there's a problem and it needs to be resolved, the question is whether or not we will take up the challenge.

However, there is another problem which needs to be dealt with. As it is we lack a major tool we require. In order for any of the changes that need to take place to happen we need quality leadership. As of right now we are a nation without leadership. Imagine a ship floating adrift in the ocean with no rudder and no sails. That ship is a pretty good representation of the state of leadership in our nation today. A leader needs to come from among the citizens, but as it stands right now there are multiple groups of citizens. We seemed to have lost our leaders when politics became an occupation for the wealthy. As stated earlier, we no longer have presidents who grew up in log cabins, now we have presidents who grew up with a silver spoon. And the few who did come from humble beginnings quickly become corrupted by the trappings of power.

Part of the problem is we no longer see democracy as being important. In fact it seems at time we take democracy for granted. We've gone from seeing voting as an indispensable part of the democratic process to viewing it as a form of entertainment. I blame the entertainment industry for this turn of events. I don't know what made television executives think that trivializing the most basic of all rights in a democracy was a good idea, but I'm starting to find this highly offensive. Over one million U.S. citizens have given their lives for this nation in combat to protect the rights we hold dear, including the right to vote. And in response the entertainment executives insult the sacrifices of our fallen heroes by equating the right to vote with pop culture. I have little doubt our founding fathers are spinning in their graves at the notion of us using our right to vote to select the next self destructive pop star. I must admit I have the desire to take Brits who created this problem and throw them into Boston Harbor just like our forefathers did with some tea.

However, as offensive as this form of entertainment is, that's not the worst of it. The real damage is still five to ten years down the line, when the children who have grown up on this type of television become of voting age. These types of shows will have conditioned young voters to see elections as popularity contests. We have enough problems with a lack of leaders as it is, but I shutter to think of the result that could come about from this mind set. What happens if we get a really charismatic individual who has some really bad ideas, but since he or she is popular they get elected? This is scary; we have television shows that are conditioning children to elect the next Adolph Hitler. Now I realize some people are going to say that I'm just using scare tactics here by connecting Hitler's name to the problem. Unfortunately that's not my intention, but rather my heart felt fear of a possible outcome. The conditions in the United States today and in the future will be prime for a dictator to come to power. We have a nation that is divided along political lines to the point where few issues ever get resolved. Whenever the war on terrorism finally ends we will see some form of recession, if not an economic depression much worse than what we're seeing now. And out of it will probably emerge some nut job pointing fingers at scapegoats. Then add into this situation a group of young impressionable voters and we have a recipe for a major political disaster. While we're clearly in need of good leaders, the last thing we need is someone who is going to lead the country down the wrong path. Honestly I'm not sure this hasn't already begun to happen.

Part of the leadership problem is the result of where we look for our leaders. We tend to pick leaders from the upper class of society. We think of these people as leaders of industry and society, but I really doubt that they have ever led anyone. We think of executives and people in positions of power as leaders, but there is a difference between a manager and a leader. If the CEO of a Fortune 500 company issues a directive I have to wonder if the employees are following the directive because the CEO is a good leader or because they want to keep their jobs. For some time now we have selected leaders from Corporate America under the misguided assumption that success in the private sector will translate into success in the public sector. The problem is that the public and private sectors are very different. The private sector functions through open competition between companies within capitalism with some companies winning and some losing. In the public sector, if two agencies compete the only loser is the citizens. The intelligence failures leading up to the terrorist attacks of September 11th provide a perfect illustration of that. The budgeting process created a condition where the NSA and the CIA were competing for funding and as a result the NSA was reluctant to share intelligence with the CIA and the CIA was reluctant to share intelligence with the NSA. Furthermore, both agencies were reluctant to share intelligence with the Department of Justice. Competition results in growth in the private sector, but in the public sector it can get people killed.

Good leaders look to serve their followers. This is a common trait we see in some of the great leaders from our nation's past. George Washington recognized the need to serve the citizens of a fragile young nation. Washington saw a nation that was vulnerable and needed to be trained. I often think of Washington's administration in terms of a political and social version of Valley Forge. In those early years when the threat of failure was always on the horizon, Washington worked to build bridges and develop consensus within the nation and abroad.

Earlier I discussed Abraham Lincoln and his concept of the United States as a "house divided". Lincoln understood that after the war was over we would have to return to being one nation, and the only way this could occur was to redevelop the bonds between the North and South. Unfortunately Lincoln never had the opportunity. Lincoln understood the grief the nation felt during the Civil War. Even the photographs taken of Lincoln as the war progressed show the terrible toll it had on him, but through it all Lincoln never lost sight of the work he was doing to lead the nation through those dark days.

One of the greatest leaders of the 20th century was Franklin Roosevelt. From the depths of the Great Depression to World War II, Roosevelt was the rock the citizens leaned on. Roosevelt conveyed the message of what it meant to be a citizen of the United States. He sought ways to connect with the citizens. Roosevelt served until his dying day, pushing past his own pain and personal demons to help our nation cope with lose and fear. He comforted the nation and showed the citizens that hope was just beyond the darkness. Our leaders don't serve, but look for us to follow. They give directions like they were sitting in a board room running a multi-billion dollar company. I don't get the sense of comfort or understanding. I don't get the sense the fights will be won and tomorrow will be better. Our leaders often talk of today or complain about yesterday.

This illustrates one of the major problems we face with any attempt to develop quality leadership in the U.S.; we've lost the ability to plan for the future. There are several reasons for this. For sometime we were unsure of the future. During the Cold War we existed under the continual specter of nuclear destruction, why bother to plan for next year when tomorrow might never arrive. The counterculture movement of the late 1960's had some impact. People took to living in the moment instead of planning for the future.

We saw the environmental problem coming, the oil crisis, the problems with illegal immigration, some of our military personnel warned about terrorism, and there are a host of other issues we knew were virtually inevitable. How many times do we have to watch as the government fails to foresee the obvious; before we, as citizens, begin to take some action to rectify the situation? And the first place to start is with real leadership. We need someone who will look to bring the nation together. We need someone who will stand up to the corporate bullies and lobbyists who are currently holding this nation hostage. We need a leader with real ideas, not pipe dreams that sound good in a five second sound bite.

Unfortunately we don't have a single politician who appears to have these qualities. Our politicians seem to be much more concerned with pointing the finger of blame at someone than actually dealing with problems themselves. To be quite honest assigning blame is easy. I would have no difficulty laying blame for 9/11 at the feet of every president from the last 50 years in some way. Laying blame is not the answer to the problem, and will do more harm than good.

Our founding fathers had some notion of the problems this nation is now facing. In fact, they saw some distinct problems and provided a solution we use everyday without knowing it. We see the Bill of Rights as the ten amendments added onto the Constitution as the ultimate guarantee of the freedoms we so dearly love. What we fail to realize is the real reason those amendments are in place. Those ten amendments represent the foundation of change. Our founding fathers realized two of the most important aspects of government. First, the fact that society's change over time and as a society changes the form of government best suited for the society must change also. The government laid out in the Constitution is well suited for a nation of 13 independent states, but it is ill suited for a nation of 50 states and numerous territories. If James Madison had been tasked with writing a document creating a government for the nation we have today it would have looked very different.

The second aspect our forefathers recognized was the need for a government to have some power. I've used this quote from Thomas Paine a number of times in this book, but it bears repeating:

> For were the impulses of conscience clear, uniform, and irresistibly obeyed, man would need no other lawgiver; but that not being the case, he finds it necessary to surrender up a part of his property to furnish means for the protection of the rest...

We create government with the intention of the citizens ceding some powers to the government so it may govern. However, our founding fathers had seen first hand the result of power and the corrupting nature of power when concentrated into the hands of a select few.

The ten amendments contained within the Bill of Rights are in place to provide the tools our forefathers deemed necessary for future generations to reshape the government to fit their society and to wrestle power away from the corrupt politicians they knew would eventually arise. As of right now we don't have need of all these tools, but if we fail to act now the day may come when the more violent tools may be needed. We owe it to future generations to ensure that day never comes. We owe it to future generations to make the changes before it's too late. If we can't trust our politicians to take the lead then it's time the citizens take the lead ourselves.

THE RIGHTS YOU HAVE AND DON'T HAVE

Before concluding I feel the need to address one more pressing issue. I've spent some considerable time discussing the ways our government has failed to provide for the citizens of the United States as required in the Constitution. However, I think there needs to be some clarifications made regarding the Bill of Rights. While I feel adamant about our need for a new Constitution, I also feel the Bill of Rights needs to stay just as it is. The ten amendments that constitute the Bill of Rights are there for some good reasons. Unfortunately, we as citizens have just forgotten (or been misguided by special interest groups, lobbyists and politicians) as to there true meaning.

There are many reasons for the Bill of Rights existing in the manner that our founding fathers created it. I wrote earlier of our founding fathers providing the Bill of Rights as a foundation for change in government, as the tools for preserving democracy. When looking at the Bill of Rights it's important to look at it as a historical document; and thus existing within a historical context. The Bill of Rights was written following the ratification of the Constitution. Our forefathers understood that they were creating a new government. Yet they still remembered the tyranny that they suffered with under the rule of the British crown. As a result the Bill of Rights serves the primary function of preventing tyranny from taking hold in the United States. The rights granted under these first ten amendments are rights that the founders recognized as being mandatory to the continuation of democratic government. In a letter to James Madison in December of 1787 Thomas Jefferson wrote, "Let me add that a bill of rights is what the people are entitled to against every government on earth, generally or particular, and what no just government should refuse or rest on inference." With this concept in mind let's take some time to look at the Bill of Rights and see what our founding fathers really meant with these ten amendments.

The First Amendments states: "Congress shall make no law respecting an establishment of religion, or prohibiting the free exercise thereof; or abridging the freedom of speech, or of the press; or the right of the people peaceably to assemble, and to petition the government for a redress of grievances." There are two distinct and separate ideas here, so let's break this down a little. The first part of this amendment deals with religion and prohibits Congress from establishing a state religion or passing any law regulating how people practice their chosen faith. It does not in any way prohibit the free expression of religion or dictate that religion is not to be part of public life. There seems to be a misunderstanding in some segments of society that this grants "freedom from religion".

In fact it could be argued that the passing of any law or legal judgment which restricts the ability of an individual to express their faith is prohibited under this amendment. The idea of religious freedom is consistent with those expressed by Thomas Jefferson in a bill on religious rights he proposed to the Virginia legislature in 1778.The second part of the First Amendment deals with the rights of freedom of speech, the press and the right to peaceful assembly. Do to some misunderstandings this part of the First Amendment has become one of the most abused parts of the Bill of Rights. When reading this section we seem to miss the end of the amendment which says "…to petition the government for a redress of grievances". This was added as a result of the desperate attempts that the colonists had made to persuade King George III to lift the taxes Parliament had levied against the colonies. Freedom of speech, the press and peaceful assembly are present in an attempt to provide the public with a voice and thus avoid another bloody revolution in the future. Freedom of the press does not give someone the right to produce child pornography or write a book describing the methods by which you manufacture methamphetamine. Freedom of speech does not give someone the right to make false accusation or threats against another human being. Freedom of assembly does not give someone the right to hold a rally promoting some ridicules racist ideology. To receive protection under the First Amendment as our forefathers wrote it the activity must be directed at the government with the intention of changing the government in some way. Anti-war protests are protected. Abortion protests are protected. Anything that is designed to get the government's attention and promote change to make the government function better is protected. Idiot paparazzi taking pictures of celebrities and making a general nuisance of them selves is not protected.

Hate to burst your bubble, but the latest pop star is not a government representative. The point here is that just because you're allowed to do something does not always mean that it's protected under the First Amendment.

The Second Amendment states: "A well regulated militia, being necessary to the security of a free state, the right of the people to keep and bear arms, shall not be infringed." This has become one of the more hotly debated amendments in the Bill of Rights because of it's application regarding gun control laws. The gun control lobby argues based on the phrase "A well regulated militia…", thus arguing that only National Guard units regulated by the states are covered by the Second Amendment. The gun lobby argues based on the phrase "… the right of the people to keep and bear arms, shall not be infringed", thus arguing that every citizen has the right to own firearms. However, the phrase "…being necessary to the security of a free state…" is the most important part and represents the idea which drove our founding fathers to include this amendment in the Bill of Rights. In the wake of the Revolutionary War our forefathers recognized the importance that the right to bear arms played in the fight for freedom. Without firearms we would never have won our independence from Britain. Furthermore, the Second Amendment acts as the final check and balance in our system of government. If the President of the United States were to disband Congress, dissolve the U.S. Supreme Court and declare himself king; then the citizens of this nation have the right under the Second Amendment to rise up using force of arms and restore democracy. The right to bear arms is the Second Amendment for a reason. At first you make your voice heard through the rights provided under the First Amendment, and if it doesn't work then the people have the right to use force to restore the elected government if necessary.

The Third Amendment states: "No soldier shall, in time of peace be quartered in any house, without the consent of the owner, nor in time of war, but in a manner to be prescribed by law." This amendment was adopted as a result of the Quartering Acts that were passed by the British Parliament prior to the revolution. Colonist saw this as an excessively heavy burden due to the owner of the house in which the soldier was staying had to provide for the soldier. It also allowed for the British Army to spy on colonial activities. Imagine how you might feel if you were told an FBI agent was going to be staying at your home and would thus be able to observe everything your family was doing. Notice there is a provision for time of war allowing the government to require citizens to house troops with the proper laws having been passed. This allows for Congress in the passing of laws for the declaration of war to make this request.

The Fourth Amendment states: "The right of the people to be secure in their persons, houses, papers, and effects, against unreasonable searches and seizures, shall not be violated, and no warrants shall issue, but upon probable cause, supported by oath or affirmation, and particularly describing the place to be searched, and the persons or things to be seized." Clearly this is the amendment providing protections against illegal search and seizures. The point here is that the people are protected from the government going in search of what ever the want in a witch hunt looking for anyone who they might be able to prosecute. While this was not a common occurrence under British rule, it did happen at times and after the Quartering Acts were passed it became a more real concern with British soldiers able to search people's homes and take evidence they found as proof of treason. The fourth Amendment has come under fire in recent years as a result of the need for intelligence to fight the War on Terrorism. One of the key points of contention in this regard is the use of broad based search warrants for wire taps. One interesting question has been raised is whether or not foreign nationals are covered under the Fourth Amendment.

The Fifth Amendment states: "No person shall be held to answer for a capital, or otherwise infamous crime, unless on a presentment or indictment of a grand jury, except in cases arising in the land or naval forces, or in the militia, when in actual service in time of war or public danger; nor shall any person be subject for the same offense to be twice put in jeopardy of life or limb; nor shall be compelled in any criminal case to be a witness against himself, nor be deprived of life, liberty, or property, without due process of law; nor shall private property be taken for public use, without just compensation." The Fifth Amendment was like the Third and Fourth Amendments in that it was an answer to the cruel and unjust treatment of colonial governors who were loyal to the British crown. The Fifth Amendment requires a grand jury indictment for major felonies with the exception of those occurring within the armed forces and militias only during time of war or unrest. We also see the prevention of double jeopardy so a defendant cannot be put on trial more than once for the same crime and protection from self incrimination. The Fifth Amendment also provides for due process and the use of eminent domain powers by the government.

The Sixth Amendment states: "In all criminal prosecutions, the accused shall enjoy the right to a speedy and public trial, by an impartial jury of the state and district wherein the crime shall have been committed, which district shall have been previously ascertained by law, and to be informed of the nature and cause of the accusation; to be confronted with the witnesses against him; to have compulsory process for obtaining witnesses in his favor, and to have the assistance of counsel for his defense." The Fifth and Six Amendments are closely tied together in that they both deal with criminal prosecution and the rights of the defendant. It was common under British rule of law for the defendant to be put in a position of being forced to testify against him or her self, but under Clause 38 of the Magna Carta, the defendant's testimony could not be the sole cause for a conviction. Furthermore, British law did not provide for a legal defense attorney in criminal proceedings. The Fifth and Sixth Amendments combined to provide for U.S. citizens the Miranda Rights that are read to individuals upon arrest today. It's also interesting to note that the idea of a "jury of one's peers" does not originate with the Bill of Rights, but rather with the Magna Carta. The Sixth Amendment only requires the jury be selected from, and the trial held, in the jurisdiction where the crime occurred.

The Seventh Amendment states: "In suits at common law, where the value in controversy shall exceed twenty dollars, the right of trial by jury shall be preserved, and no fact tried by a jury, shall be otherwise reexamined in any court of the United States, than according to the rules of the common law." In general this amendment deals with matters of civil litigation. The reason for the Seventh Amendment being in place was to prevent the rich and elite from taking advantage of friendships with judges who might decide civil matters. By retaining the right to a jury trial in civil courts all citizens are guaranteed an impartial decision. In a way the Seventh Amendment also helps to give rise to the small claims courts in use today. The Seventh Amendment further lays out the conditions under which a verdict in a civil court can be appealed.

The Eighth Amendment states: "Excessive bail shall not be required, nor excessive fines imposed, nor cruel and unusual punishments inflicted." With the rise of capital punishment, the Eighth Amendment has come under intense scrutiny. It's clear from historical accounts that cruel punishment was the norm under British rule. However, there is clear indication that George Washington also used these same forms of punishment in disciplining troops during the Revolutionary War. We also have an issue with the prohibition of excessive bail and fines. It would seem that what would be considered excessive would be determined based on the economic status of the individual. What is excessive for a multimillionaire is far different in comparison to what is excessive for a person working a minimum wage job. None the less our lawmakers have managed to go overboard on this issue. Proof of these excessive fines can be seen in the form of the FBI warning at the beginning of a home movie.

The Ninth Amendment states: "The enumeration in the Constitution, of certain rights, shall not be construed to deny or disparage others retained by the people." Simply put the Ninth Amendment says that the rights listed in the Constitution are not to be used to deny the people of rights they already have. The Ninth Amendment functions in two different ways. First, the rights that are provided to the people in the Bill of Rights and the rights provided to the United States government and to governments of individual states cannot be used to deprive the citizens of their rights.

Secondly, the Ninth Amendment prohibits us from amending the Constitution to take away someone's rights. This means that in reality, the 18th Amendment imposing prohibition of alcohol was unconstitutional even before it was overturned by the 21st Amendment. Furthermore, for all of you looking to ban gay marriage, you better find a way to nullify the Ninth Amendment first.

And finally the Tenth Amendment states: "The powers not delegated to the United States by the Constitution, nor prohibited by it to the states, are reserved to the states respectively, or to the people." The Tenth Amendment best summarizes the purpose behind the Bill of Rights. The Tenth Amendment forces decentralization of power by prohibiting the United States government from taking powers they have not been given by the people. Our forefathers did not want the same situation which developed under a monarchy to occur here. The founding fathers believed that by spreading the power out so it wasn't concentrated in one branch or level of government helped to prevent any one group from becoming too powerful. The only powers the Federal government has are the powers granted in Article Four of the United States Constitution. Now for some reason that has eluded me, members of Congress seem to think the Tenth Amendment doesn't apply to them. If Congress wants the power to pass laws regulating issues that are not delegated to them in the Constitution, then I would suggest they amend the Constitution so that the laws are legal. Until then I wish the U.S. Supreme Court would stop being lazy and start throwing some of these unconstitutional laws out.

So that in a nut shell is the Bill of Rights and chances are the real meaning behind those ten amendments are far different then what you've been told in the past. The idea behind the Bill of Rights is to ensure the rights of the people are never used to hurt the people. Our forefathers realized that the best way to ensure this was to make sure the people's ability to run their government was never taken away. Once the people start losing their rights, the process of democratic government is soon to follow.

With all of this said, let me make something as clear as possible: regardless of whether they are

a Democrat, a Republican, or someone else all together, if anyone tries to get you to vote for them based on a policy that requires the revocation of one of the Ten Amendments contained within the Bill of Rights, DO NOT VOTE FOR THEM! I don't care if they promise you peace on earth and millions of dollars, DO NOT VOTE FOR THEM!

Furthermore, if you don't believe in the rights guaranteed to citizens of the United State by these Ten Amendments; then I would suggest you need to leave this country. If you don't believe in the right of the citizens to hold free elections and practice all of the other aspects of democratic government, then once again I would suggest you leave this country. If you believe the United States should be governed under religious laws or by a theocratic government, then I would suggest you leave this country. If you believe the citizens of the United States of America should give up the rights our forefathers fought for just so you can feel more at home, then you need to get out of this country.

CONCLUSION

There is no real difference between the various parties across the political landscape. All politicians, regardless of their party affiliation, are out for the same goal: power. Now, this power comes in all different forms, but no matter what form it takes power in terms of politics tends to always breed politicians who are greedy for more. Being a state representative isn't enough, they want to be a U.S. Senator and eventually President of the United States. We as a nation need to come to terms with greed as an illness. I have yet to see any other illness that can cause as much pain and suffering as greed. Wars often begin because of greed. Poverty is in some ways the result of greed. It could easily be argued that greed is the root cause of every significant problem facing the United States today. I've already demonstrated the greed existing in our corporate culture today.

146

I talked earlier about fixing the problems right the first time. Greed is a problem that our forefathers understood all too clear. The greed of King George III and the British Parliament was part of what led to the Revolution, as they were unwilling to cede any power to the colonies. When people gain power, they're unwillingness to compromise it almost inevitably leads to conflict and often times that
means war. More often then not, it's the powerless, not the powerful, who lose in wars.

Our politicians become corrupt because they are greedy for power. As I've displayed throughout this book, there are solutions to the problems facing our nation. The question we need to ask is why our elected officials are not coming up with some of the solutions? To put it simply, politicians are not interested in finding solutions. Politicians are more than happy to point out the problem, exacerbate the problem and in some cases even create a whole new set of problems. Rarely however will you see a politician solving a problem. The reason for politicians being so reluctant to solve problems is clear. The more problems there are, the more topics they have for their political campaigns.

The citizens can't wait or trust the politicians to fix these problems. It seems inevitable for politicians to engage in whatever tactics they deem necessary to gain political office and the power their elected office entails. It's time for the citizen of the United States to regain control of the future of our nation for ourselves and the generations to come. I discussed earlier the responsibility we all have as citizens to the future success of this nation. If you have any doubt regarding this responsibility then I challenge you to look no further than a history book. A lot of the wars our nation has fought have been to prevent a future generation from having to fight it. Perfect examples are the Revolutionary War, the Civil War and World War II. I for one am thankful those former generations took it upon themselves to deal with some of those issues.

The question we as citizens need to be asking is, "What can I do to help?" The best thing any citizen can do is to become as active as possible in YOUR government. By being more involved in government, the citizens force more accountability on politicians. Politicians have come to believe that with power comes a certain amount of freedom from accountability, but nothing could be further from the truth. As citizens we are inundated with the idea that we are the best nation in the world, then why are we settling for second rate government?

Being active also means being informed. It's a lot harder for politicians to hide stuff from the citizens if the citizens know what is going on in the first place. Let me clarify this point. When I say be informed, I don't mean read the newspaper or watch TV. The fact is the media is biased. Fox News can claim to be "Fair and Balanced" all they want, and if you believe it I have some international landmarks to sell you. Attend city council meetings, focus groups with your member of Congress, watch CSPAN and read about bills being voted on in Congress. When someone is running for political office learn everything you can about that person, good and bad, then make a decision. I'm not going to trust the Republican presidential candidate to tell me the truth about his Democratic opponent or vice versa. The only way you will find the truth is to look for the truth.

In the course of this book I have done my best to stay clear of partisan politics. The work of fixing the United States is not a partisan issue. Partisan bickering is a major component in the problems and will definitely not play a role in any of the solutions. However to illustrate my point regarding politicians saying what people want to hear in order to get elected, I will take issue with one. And that one is Barack Obama. Now, I'm picking President Obama for a reason, mainly because he illustrates all the problems I have discussed regarding politicians. While I could go and take issue with almost everything about how he came to be elected, I will limit myself to the whole Radical Reverend Wright debacle.

Now I will be the first to defend the Radical Reverend's right to speak his mind in a religious context as provided in the First Amendment. With that stated I completely disagree with his hate filled comments which serve no other purpose than attempting to set back the civil rights movement a few decades. Furthermore, I don't take issue President Obama because of the Radical Reverend's comments, but because of President Obama's lack of action regarding the comments. As a Christian, if I heard a minister say those kinds of comments I would get up and walk out of the church. I've discussed this before, Christian doctrine states that "of one blood God created all men". I could not sit in a church and claim belief in Christ as my Lord and Savior and believe the hate filled messages preached by Reverend Wright.

This brings me to my concern about President Obama. I could care less what a politician's religious stance is, as long as they are a good leader. However, if a politician is going to take a stance on religion then they need to make sure they stand by the ideals of their religion. From my perspective it now looks like President Obama simply used Christianity as an element within his campaign and I'm wondering if he it truthful in his

149

faith. I honestly don't know where he stands on his faith. It could be that he is very strong in his faith or for him faith is simply a means for getting more votes. Unfortunately his actions have caused me to question this issue.

I hope President Obama is truthful in his faith, but for a moment let's assume he's not and it was just an act to gain votes. What are the implications of a politician lying about something like faith? We should find it deeply disturbing for someone to lie about such a personal matter as faith. Faith is one of the driving forces behind how we interact with the world around us. Most of the decisions I make on a daily basis are in some way driven by my faith. If someone will lie about their faith, what else will they lie about? I want to make this clear again that I'm not saying President Obama is not a devout Christian, because I have no idea how serious he is in regards to his faith. What I do know is that the uncertainty with which he reacted to the remarks made by Reverend Wright make me question his integrity. The definition of integrity is to do the right thing no matter the personal consequences. President Obama appears to have been willing to sacrifice his integrity for the opportunity to advance his political career.

Now I realize that there are many people reading this wondering why this matters so much, and why I'm spending time talking about this issue that took place some years ago. I'm sure there are many of President Obama's supporters who are thinking I need to simply let the issue of Rev. Wright's comments die. I ask the good reader to bear with me for a moment while I try to explain the other side of this coin so to speak.

Let's take a moment to remove the controversy from its current context and look at it from the perspective of some other historical figures. While the situations are clearly not the same, there are some lessons that can be learned from historical figures on this account. The results of political leaders who place personal goals and career aspirations ahead of their integrity is nothing new. As a nation we have seen this scenario play out time and again over our collective history. How many Watergate's do we as a nation need to see before we begin holding politicians accountable for their personal integrity?

I honestly think President Obama says what ever he thinks people want to hear at a given moment. President Obama claimed he was going to utilize the internet based system he had in place to accept small campaign contributions from supporters. The logic behind this move seemed to be for President Obama's campaign to claim "voice of the people" status over these contributions. I have a question: how do we know these small contributions were not in reality large contributions that came from major corporations and special interest groups who were using the internet to get around campaign finance limits by using other people's names. After all, this is the internet where you can pretend to be anyone you wish. It seems to me President Obama was less concerned with what is in the best interest of the people and more concerned with how he could exploit a loop hole in the current campaign finance laws to better his chances of gaining office. Wow, look at that we're right back here at a politician selling out their integrity to get ahead and gain more power.

Once again let me emphasis that I'm not in any way supporting one part or the other. Obama is a much easier target for these problems because of the way he changes his stance on the issues. As often as President Obama changes his tune he must have a large account with iTunes. In fact, it's not a issue with President Obama alone, we could even go so far as to create the term "iPaigning" to describe the manner in which politicians change their stance on a moments notice, just like shuffling though the songs on an mp3 player. It is extremely bad foreign policy to take a stance on an issue and then do a public about face on the same issue a few days later. It plays havoc with the consumer confidence when the consumers have no concrete plans for the future. To be quite honest I feel the matter in which President Obama keeps changing his stance on issues is nothing more than a clear demonstration of President Obama's lack of self confidence in his own decisions.

These problems have persisted for far too long in our nation, and it is up to the citizens to bring this problem to a swift and decisive end. There is no way for us to begin fixing problems as long as the people trusted to run our government are lying to us. To further add to the problem we have to decipher the lies from the truth we hear from the media. When it's not plagiarism, or manufacturing documents to prove a phony story; the media will simply decide what they don't wish to report or fail to report the entire story in other cases. The sad reality is our western news is little different from that of the nationalist controlled media in China. The only difference being in China it's the government controlling what is reported where here in the U.S. it's the media outlets themselves reporting only what will benefit their bottom line. We can't trust the politicians to makes the changes and we can't trust the media to report the need for changes, so who do we turn to?

What superhero will come to rescue us from the mess that has been created by the elite of society?

I say we turn to the greatest superhero of all: the United States citizens. This great nation was founded by the citizens who risked everything they had for the prospect of a better future. Our nation is defended by citizen soldiers who risk everything for a brighter tomorrow in a safer world. Everyday citizens in this nation go to work at jobs where their lives are put in danger so their fellow citizens may be free from harm. I ask you; take a moment someday to think about where you would be and what your life would be like without those citizens and many others who spend their days changing the live of complete strangers. Looking at the fortitude of the United States citizen how can there be any doubt that we as a nation have the power, drive and ability in us to change the course of this nation to ensure a brighter tomorrow?

I have little doubt there are some citizens in this nation willing to take a stand and fight to fix the problems. Unfortunately, I see a lot of citizens who seem content with President Obama without any regard for whether or not he's the best person for the job.

As I've stated before, I dislike Republicans and Democrats pretty equally. If anything I might dislike Democrats a little more because of their deceitful nature. Let me explain my personal thoughts on the difference between a Republican and a Democrat. A Republican will lie to you to get your money. No matter what it takes, they want more money. They're greedy as can be, and will do what ever is necessary to get money. Democrats are greedy too, don't get me wrong. The difference is Democrats don't want money, they want power.

Where Republicans see political office as a means to make money off of lobbying and other activities; Democrats see political office as a gateway to power. And just like their Republican counterparts, Democrats will do what ever it takes to get power. They're both greedy, they just have different goals. Quite frankly, the Democrats bother me a little more than the Republicans in regards to their goals. As far as I'm concerned the Republicans can have all the money they want, they always seem to find more, and eventually they will find a way to self destruct. However, as I stated earlier, there is only so much power to go around, and if the Democrats want to gain more power they have to take it from somewhere. Unfortunately this means the power gets taken from the citizens. But, just like the Republicans, the Democrats will eventually self destruct under their own greed, the difference being the amount of damage that they do to society before their self destruction occurs. In this politicians are generally the same, they tend to be so greedy that if you give them enough rope they will eventually hang themselves.

I don't consider myself to be a Republican or a Democrat. Granted I tend to vote Republican more times than not, but mainly because of the issue of gun control. There's something about power hungry Democrats wanting to take away the right of the people to bear arms for the protection of their constitutionally guaranteed rights that really bothers me. I do however consider myself to be a pissed off citizen of the United States of America. I'm pissed of with how poorly my fellow citizens are treated. I'm pissed off with the way we are lied to by the media. I'm pissed off with the way discrimination is tolerated in certain instances. I'm pissed off that the welfare of the citizens has taken a backseat to the profit margins of big business.

The one thing that pisses me off more than anything else is the fact that our politicians are the biggest obstacle to progress our nation faces. Let's face it; politicians have a vested interest in maintaining the status quo. I've stated this before but it bears repeating: if politicians actually fixed problems and made good on their promises they would have nothing to campaign about. In order to continue campaigning on the bases of meaningless promises the problems have to continue. It amazes me how every election I hear the same promises from the same political parties, and yet the promises never ring true. However, I'm even more amazed that we keep electing the same liars each election.

If I could get only one idea from this book across to the political leadership of The United States it would be this: we're feed up. We are tired of being caught as the pawns in your pathetic little political games. Is it really that hard to put your own petty power plays aside and do what is in the best interest of the citizens who elected you? I hate to be the one to break this to all the politicians, lobbyists and activists out there, but doing the right thing doesn't always mean everyone is going to be happy. If my car needs a new exhaust system I'm not happy about spending the money on it, but I know it's the right thing to do to help protect the environment.

Our politicians have become completely consumed by their own greed. I shudder to think of the billions of dollars that have been raised since 2007 for political campaigns. How many lives could have been saved if that money had been used for medical research? How many lives could have been made better with that money? Instead, the politicians placate us; they tell us how they feel for us and understand our needs and concerns. However, the amounts of money they are willing to spend to gain power and fortune off the backs of the U.S. citizens betray their real intentions.

For all the short comings we have in our government, I know the future can be better. When I look back on our nation's history and think about all we have endured I can't help but have hope. In fact, it might be best to say I have faith. I know, faith is a dirty word when it comes to government, but the way I see it faith is what will see our nation through these troubling times. I have faith some group of citizens will take a stand for what is right, take a stand for justice. I have faith some group of citizens will decided to make a difference and take up the mantle of leadership in one of their nation's darkest hours. I have faith the future will be better. I have faith in the Citizens of the United States of America.

POST SCRIPT:
RELIGION AND DEMOCRACY

DISCLAIMER: At no point in this book have I attempted to hide my faith in Jesus Christ as my Lord and Savior. However, up until this point I have attempted to write in terms all citizens can connect with regardless of their stance on religion. I fully respect the rights of all religions to practice as they see fit as afforded them in the First Amendment. With this stated, in discussing community involvement I only have the model of Christianity to draw on. It is not my intention to put down any other religion or attempt to convert people to my beliefs. If in reading this some people are convinced to take Christ as their personal savior then praise be to God that it happened, but God's will not my own be done.

Some where along the way we came up with this ridicules notion that there must be an absolute separation between government and religion of any form, so let me straighten this issue out a little. It is absolutely impossible to completely separate the government from religion. The government, in its legislative function, acts as the nation's moral compass. The morals which result in laws being passed are based in some why, shape, or form on religious beliefs. This is not to say we should have a national religion, because we absolutely shouldn't. However, completely banning any expression of faith within the corridors of government is ludicrous.

Religion plays a very important role in society. Unfortunately we've lost sight of religions importance. Our nation started out because of people fleeing Europe in search of religious freedom. Now, if you say a prayer in public you have to fear ridicule from someone who claims to be offended. I use the word "claims" on purpose, because I personally don't believe most of these individuals are actually offended. I do believe they are looking for their fifteen minutes of fame and will attack any religion they can in order to get it. I for one don't care if they get offended by my faith. Christ warned his followers that we would be hated for our belief in him, but gave us comfort in the reminder that they hated him first.

This is not to say religion in the United States today is devoid of short comings. It appears to me that there are a lot of ministers out there preaching in the name of Jesus Christ, when they clearly failed to actually read the New Testament. I hear ministers on television complaining about how this group or that group is going to suffer eternal damnation because of their sins. I guess some of us forgot the passage about "judge not lest ye be judged". To put this as simply as I can, if you're passing judgment about who is or isn't going to heaven; then I want to see the nail holes in your hands. Christ is the only one with that power. Christ died on the cross, rose again on the third day and ascended to heaven to sit at the right hand of his Father. Come judgment day, Christ will sit in judgment over all the peoples, kings and nations of the world.

Now I'm not saying there isn't such a thing as sin, there absolutely is. What I am saying is no individual on planet Earth has the right to decide whether or not another person has sinned. I read the Bible and based on my reading I decide there are certain acts God says are sins, and as a result I choose not to take part in those activities. At the same time, I'm not going to sit back and try to force my beliefs on others. The religious community needs to come to terms with the idea of individuals having free will, and have been granted free will by God. God does not want people to have faith because they are forced to. As Christ himself said, "may will be called, but few will be chosen." God wants individuals to enter into eternal life by making a conscious decision to live righteously.

Christianity has an unofficial place within our system of government. In 2 Corinthians 3:17 we're told "Now the Lord is the Spirit, and where the Spirit of the Lord is, there is liberty." Our sense of freedom is derived directly from Christianity. If we can be free from sin in heaven by taking Christ as our savior and living in the spirit, then why not be free on earth in the flesh? However, this concept is what can cause us problems abroad. If a nation doesn't believe in Christ and the remission of sin, how are we to convey the concept of freedom in terms they can understand? The only way to accomplish this goal is to learn about other cultures and then relate the concept of freedom in terms they can understand. Then, hopefully after democracy has taken hold will the idea of Christianity will begin to flourish.

If you are going to use religion to fight a political battle, then you need to make sure that you don't sound like a hypocrite. For example, if you insist on fighting against abortion claiming life is sacred, then don't stand on the side of capital punishment. I truly don't understand how anyone claiming to believe in Jesus Christ can be in favor of capital punishment. When I think of the early church leaders who were executed for believing in Christ, it makes me shudder to think of capital punishment. Even today there are areas in the world where people are executed for believing in Christianity. If you are a Christian and you believe in capital punishment I ask you this simple question: when Pontius Pilate offered to free Jesus as he had done nothing worthy of crucifixion, how would you have voted? If you had been in the crowd, what would you have been yelling?

It is my personal belief that a person should be given all the time they need to come to know Jesus Christ. Peter asked Christ if he should forgive his brother up to seven times, and Christ replied that he should forgive him as many times as were necessary. If a person commits murder, then yes they should be put in prison. But if Saul could be converted on the road to Damascus, then surely if it is the will of God, a murderer can be converted in a prison cell. However, if you execute a murderer before it happens, you've potentially denied him or her the opportunity to know Christ. Christ said there will be more joy in heaven over one sinner who repents that for 99 righteous people who didn't need to repent.

The whole idea of doing unto others and loving your neighbor is about this very issue. Murder isn't wrong because it ended someone's life. After all, scripture tells us if a person doesn't believe in Christ their already dead in the flesh. Rather, the reason murder is wrong is because it denies someone the opportunities they need to come to know Christ as their savior. What bigger stumbling block can you put in someone's path than to cut their journey short? Just as we are all of one body with Christ, we are one nation. Each citizen makes up a different part of the body of U.S. citizens. Each person has a different function, but all of the functions are important. When we see our nation from this perspective it becomes clear that people who are in prison are not criminals so much as sick and injured parts of the whole body. Would you consider amputating your index finger over a paper cut? Surely not. We need to find ways to treat these conditions within our society in a manner fitting Christianity.

It also seems fitting that the new breed of leaders our nation is in desperate need of comes from a background of Christianity. We need servant leaders who understand that sometimes the leader must make sacrifices in order to help their followers; just as Christ sacrificed himself for us on the cross. This is not to say these new leaders need to bully people into believing in Christianity, and I know some misguided minister out there is going to take it that way. What it does mean is these ideals which can be taken from Christianity and applied to leadership should be taught. We need to teach these new leaders two very important tasks: how to choose their battles and how to fight their battles.

First off there are some battles which are worth fighting and some which aren't. For example, when I was a college student I took two courses dealing with the theory of evolution. I found the topic very interesting and did well in the classes. However, I know this is going to give some anthropologists' and paleontologists' heart attacks, but the fact of the matter is I don't care. Whether humans evolved from apes or were created as the Old Testament says does not change my faith in God. Maybe the fossils were put there by Satan to confuse us. Maybe God provided the Adam and Eve story because the idea of evolution was too complicated for earlier civilizations to understand. The fact is at the end of the day it doesn't change the type of person I will be tomorrow. In the New Testament it says if you live in the flesh, you die in the flesh, but if you live in the spirit you will have eternal life. Arguing about evolution is arguing a matter of the flesh, and I personally prefer to live in the spirit as Christ suggested. The argument for or against evolution will not change a person's belief in the existence of God. If a person believes they will continue to believe regardless of the fossil evidence. But if you ban the teaching of evolution it makes it seem like you're hiding something and will push the non-believers even further away.

During his ministry on earth Christ seems to have understood the need to pick which battles to fight. When the temple elders tested Jesus about paying taxes to Caesar, Christ replied "render unto Caesar the things that are Caesar's and to God those things that are God's". This is by no means to suggest Christ supported the immoral things Caesar was doing with the tax money. Christ understood the day to fight that battle would come at the Second Coming. Knowing what battles to fight is largely about knowing the resources at hand and what the best use for the resources is. Christ wasn't concerned with using the resources his Father had provided to him to fight Caesar, but rather to save the souls of his followers. A prime example of this is seen when Jesus is arrested and he instructs Peter to sheath his sword. Jesus knows that he can call on his Father to send angels to fight, but if that happened then the work Christ was sent to perform would not have been accomplished.

Some battles are clearly worth fighting. An example of one of these battles would be abortion. This brings us to the second of these two important tasks: how to fight the battle. It's a mistake to fight abortion by passing judgment on people and call them murderers. There are two reasons why this tactic is a mistake. First, passing judgment in the name of Christianity makes your argument look hypocritical. Secondly, calling someone a murderer is never a good way to win people over to your side. Thus it makes sense to fight the battle with tactics consistent with the teachings of Jesus Christ. When the elders and chief priests of the temple came to Christ asking where his authority came from, Christ responded by asking them where John the Baptist's baptism was from. The elders and chief priests were left unable to answer. This same tactic can be used against abortion advocates. Instead of arguing from the pro-life stance, become pro-choice yourselves. Make this argument: if two people make the choice to have sexual relations, and they make the choice to not use the appropriate amount of protection, then they are making the choice to have a child. This argument takes away the idea of judgment and abortion being murder and instead places emphasis on being responsible for ones actions. Being responsible for your actions is an idea consistent with the teachings of Christ. After all what else is repenting of your sins but taking responsibility for the unrighteous things you've done and asking for forgiveness.

It also helps to take the fight out of religious terms in some cases. Instead of making abortion a matter of morality, make it an issue of civics. Frame abortion in terms of taking responsibility for your actions. Society is based in part on the realization that decisions have consequences, some good and some bad. If you commit a crime you pay the consequences. If you make bad decisions you deal with the results. So why should it be any different for pregnancy? We have people going overseas to adopt children because the waiting lists are so long here. We have terrorists who want to kill U.S. citizens, and someone wants to prevent a citizen from coming into this world? When abortion is used as a form of birth control it is an act of selfishness.

Clearly, these arguments don't apply to cases where abortions are done because a mother's life is in danger, rape, incest, and so forth. In those cases I would suggest we look back to the earlier issue of judgment and let the decision be between a woman, her doctor and God. I don't see God holding someone accountable for something they had no control over. For God to hold a person accountable in that way would no be consistent with the same God who sent his son to die for the sins of mankind.

Leaders need to learn to serve their followers first. Jesus Christ is easily the most successful leader the world has ever seen. But Christ didn't come and make demands of people, instead he came and served his future followers on the cross. Christ was very aware of the example he was presenting to those who believed in him and he conveyed this idea to his disciples. In 1st Corinthians Chapter 9, Paul says, "For though I am free from all men, I have made myself a servant to all, that I might win the more...". We need to train leaders who will begin to follow this line of thinking, acting as servants to their followers as opposed to rulers. Setting a good example is one of the most important aspects of leadership.

I personally gave up drinking alcohol a number of years ago. I didn't have a problem drinking alcohol; in fact I rarely drank to begin with. For me drinking became more of a spiritual problem. I didn't like the feeling of being in a bar and knowing that my decision to drink might have a negative impact on someone else. Say someone walks into the same bar where I'm drinking and seeing everyone else drinking he orders a beer. Unknown to me and everyone else in the bar this person is in a 12 step program trying to beat his addiction to alcohol. Granted, he should have stayed away from the bar in the first place, but still I figure I just helped to put a stumbling block in his path. Had I been drinking something other than alcohol the outcome might have been different.

I provide this example to illustrate the point that good leadership often means placing the needs of the many before your own. If a leader is only concerned with their own needs or places their needs first, they will lose followers every time. When we read the story of Christ feeding the multitudes, Christ always breaks the bread and distributes it to the people, we never read of him eating the food first. During the Last Supper, Christ blesses the bread and the wine, and then gives it to his disciples. No where does it say that he ate of it first, but rather it is meant to be symbolic of the fact that Christ was giving his body for the sins of many. The act of taking communion is about remembering how our leader put the needs of our souls before his own.

The idea of selfless leadership is epitomized in one of the most quoted scriptures in the New Testament, John 3:16: "For God so loved the world that he gave his only begotten son that those who believe in him shall not perish, but have eternal life." God put the needs of us, his followers, before his own by sending his son to die for our sins. More than that, God had faith that some of us would accept his son as our savior. Great leaders have faith in their followers and show this faith by putting the needs of their followers first.

In the conclusion to this book I spoke of the destructive nature of greed. The ultimate example of greed is when someone places their own needs before the needs of others. This is one of the big ticket ideas within the Bible. Most sin originates from greed and by connection selfishness. If a leader is willing to put the needs of the followers first, then the followers will help support the leader. If a person will trust in God and give up greed and selfish gains, then God will provide what the person needs.

This form of leadership would save a lot of businesses. Instead of cutting employees, have the company leadership take a pay cut. The effect is the employees see the leadership making sacrifices for the employees and as a result they are willing to work harder to help turn the company around.

Faith can be a difficult concept for a leader to come to term with. It often seems counterintuitive for a leader to give over control to faith as opposed to controlling things for him or her self. However, by trusting God to provide guidance, many of the decisions you will make will become easier. Faith proves to be the ultimate tool in a leader's toolbox, and the most powerful force in a person's life.